THE SAGA OF
CIMBA

THE SAGA OF
CIMBA

Richard Maury

With drawings by the author

Introduction by Jonathan Raban

INTERNATIONAL MARINE / McGRAW-HILL

Camden, Maine • New York • San Francisco • Washington, D.C. •
Auckland • Bogotá • Caracas • Lisbon • London • Madrid • Mexico City •
Milan • Montreal • New Delhi • San Juan • Singapore • Sydney •
Tokyo • Toronto

Other titles in The Sailor's Classics series:
Gipsy Moth Circles the World, *Francis Chichester*
40,000 Miles in a Canoe and Sea Queen, *John C. Voss*
The Strange Last Voyage of Donald Crowhurst, *Tomalin and Hall*

International Marine
A Division of The McGraw-Hill Companies

10 9 8 7 6 5 4 3 2 1
Copyright © 1971, 2001 Lynn Maury
Introduction © 2001 Jonathan Raban

Originally published in USA 1939 by Harcourt, Brace and Company and in
Great Britain by George G. Harrap & Co., Ltd.
Published in 1971 by John de Graff, Inc.

Library of Congress Cataloging-in-Publication Data

Maury, Richard.
    The saga of Cimba / Richard Maury, with drawings by the author ;
introduction by Jonathan Raban.
        p.   cm.
    Originally published: New York : Harcourt, Brace, and Co., c1939.
    ISBN 0-07-137225-3 (alk. paper)
    1. Maury, Richard—Journeys. 2.Voyages and travels. 3. Cimba (Schooner)
I. Title.
    G530.M45 2000
    910.4'5—dc21

Printed on 55# Sebago by R. R. Donnelley, Crawfordsville, IN
Design by Dennis Anderson
Page layout by Publishers' Design and Production Services, Inc.
Production management by Janet Robbins

In Memory of

Carrol Hyde Huddleston

Russell "Dombey" Dickinson

Warren Heisler

George M. Taggart

*Valiant companions who aided and
urged the* Cimba *over her trek*

CONTENTS

INTRODUCTION TO THE SAILOR'S CLASSICS EDITION
JONATHAN RABAN

THE SAGA OF CIMBA is one of the tiny handful of small-boat voyages that belong in the larger pantheon of the literature of the sea. Though it's the only book that Richard Maury ever published, it is the work of a vastly gifted and original writer who stands tall enough to be at ease in the company of Dana, Melville, Conrad, and Masefield.

It is the business of art to make sense and pattern from the chaos of life, so it should come as no great surprise to learn that the shapely, word-perfect *Saga of Cimba* found its raw material in a three-year voyage that would appear to have been a long, shapeless catalogue of accidents—some of them dreadful ones. In 1933, Maury and his friend Carrol Huddleston, both young but experienced sailors, bought a tiny Nova Scotian fishing schooner, named her *Cimba*, and planned to sail around the world. The voyage was to be an escape from the austerities of the Great Depression into the (as it was then) remote, exotic, and romantic world of the South Seas and beyond. Long-distance small-boat voyaging was still a relative novelty in 1933, though the adven-

tures of Joshua Slocum, John Voss, Alain Gerbault, and
W. A. Robinson, among others, had already given shape
and precedent to young men's dreams of running away to
sea as captains of their own pint-sized sailing craft.

In Nova Scotia, they took on a local hand, Warren
Heisler, and set off to refit the boat in Stamford, Connecticut, close to Maury's home. On this first trip, *Cimba* came
within inches of being lost to the rocks off Cape Cod in a fe-
rocious onshore gale. Less than two weeks later, Warren
Heisler (who had signed on for the round-the-world voyage)
was swept to his death from another Nova Scotian fishing
boat. Ten days after Heisler's drowning, Huddleston died
when he lost his footing while tending *Cimba* in Stamford
harbor during a November storm. Maury found another
companion—the taciturn "Dombey" Dickinson—and, very
late in the season, the two men sailed from New York,
bound for Bermuda. While Dickinson and Maury were
searching the horizon for the landfall of the Bermudan islands, *Cimba* was hit by hurricane-force winds that drove
her far west into the North Atlantic, where the confused and
toppling seas sank three much larger craft in *Cimba*'s immediate vicinity. The boat—lucky to survive—was laid up
for three months in Bermuda, before setting off again for the
Panama Canal and the South Seas.

That part of the voyage went well, though every small
boat is an emotional pressure-cooker, and in *Cimba*'s
cramped cabin (a Bermudan newspaperman described it as

having 4'8" headroom and "only one proper bunk") there were, as Maury delicately intimates, troubling tensions between himself and his gruff crew. They arrived in Tahiti, where *Cimba* spent eight—apparently idle—months, then continued her broken journey westward across the Pacific, with a third man, George Taggart, now on board (three men in a bunk!). At the beginning of September 1935, *Cimba* was wrecked in Fiji, on Suva Reef, towed off, extensively rebuilt, and refloated a month later. In December, she was painted with government-issue copper anti-fouling, which turned out to be worse than useless, since in March 1936, she was found to be riddled with worm. Again she was rebuilt, and was ready to pick up the thread of the journey in August 1936. Dickinson and Taggart had left, and Maury planned to take on a paid hand; a Fijian teenage boy named Joela. At this point the Fijian government became involved, though the exact facts of the matter are obscured in a bureaucratic fog worthy of the beginning of Dickens's *Bleak House*. *Cimba* was impounded by the authorities (she became the official yacht of the Governor of Fiji, so it is said); Maury fell seriously ill, and left Fiji three months later, as a passenger on a steamer, watching his boat—now government property—lie placidly at anchor.

Put like that, the events of the voyage would seem to defy the efforts of the most ingenious storyteller to shape them into any kind of coherent narrative—still less a book as happy, as irrepressibly buoyant in spirit as *The Saga of Cimba*, which, far from being (as one might reasonably expect) a Conradian tale of sorrows and human folly, is the most eloquent prose hymn ever written to the exhilaration, the beauty, and the sheer joy of being at sea. Yet it is precisely because the voyage was so fraught with difficulty and tragedy, and Maury had to work so hard to reconcile the disasters that befell him with his steadfast love of the sea, that the book rings true. The joy is real, but it is wrested from the teeth of experience by a writer of quite extraordinary skill, cunning, and determination.

AT FIRST GLANCE, you might think that the book's title puts it squarely in the shopworn tradition of *cruise-of* narratives—*The Cruise of* . . . the *Tomtit* . . . the *Kate* . . . the *Alerte* . . . the *Snark* . . . the *Nona* . . . the *Teddy* . . . all books in which the name of the boat is a *faux*-modest mask for the human adventures of the authors (respectively, Wilkie Collins, E. E. Middleton, E. F. Knight, Jack London, Hilaire Belloc, and Erling Tambs). But *The Saga of Cimba* is not like that at all. First, it's a true saga, in the Icelandic mold; a succession of heroic endeavors worthy of Gunnarr or Grettir. Second, *Cimba* really is its heroine—and Maury manages to pull off that feat without the faintest trace of whimsy.

He subordinates himself and his crewmembers to the role of attendants to the schooner. It is often only their hands that we see—the hand on the tiller, or the sail, attached to no particular owner. We know the hand belongs to Dombey only because the smell of his pipe smoke is in the air. When someone dies, or quits the boat, or when resentful argument breaks out among the crew, the event is recorded with such laconic brevity that an inattentive reader might miss it altogether. The epitaphs on Heisler and Huddleston are brief, solemn, and to the point. The men are barely mentioned again, because this is not their story, it is *Cimba*'s.

In a striking phrase that occurs in the first and in the penultimate paragraph, *Cimba* is seen "as though cut of fragile porcelain on the sea," and that image haunts the book. Maury might as well have launched a fine and precious Sèvres vase on the water, exposing it to the upreared wave, the flattening wind, the jagged scrape of rock and coral, marveling all the while over its survival in the wilderness of ocean. Having largely excluded himself and his own concerns from the book (it is typical of his manner that when *Cimba* passes "the lonely white form of the *Tusitala*," one of the last working square-riggers, in New York Harbor, Maury does not see fit to mention that his own sea-apprenticeship was served on board that ship—just as when *Cimba* arrives in Bermuda he neglects to say that he spent his boyhood there), he is free to watch the progress of his bone-china boat with an intense, unswerving concentration, as rapt and self-forgetful as any scientist at a microscope.

At one point Maury claims Joseph Conrad as his "secret patron saint," but this shy salute only serves to underline how very differently Conrad and Maury write of the sea. With Conrad, the reader is almost invariably looking down at the water from the deck or bridge of a ship, and the sea is rarely center stage: it is the backdrop to the action of Conrad's maritime novels—seen in brief glimpses, or in the occasional glowing set piece, while the real business of the novel is with its human characters. Only in *Typhoon* is the sea met full-face, in all its appalling glory. With Maury, the perspective is entirely changed: the reader finds himself very nearly level with the sea, with the water only inches from his nose, and the waves breaking more often overhead than underfoot. With Maury, too, the sea—or rather the fascinating, complex intercourse between *Cimba* and the sea—is the subject. All the drama of the book takes place along the boat's waterline, while the people aboard her are of interest only to the degree to which they can assist the boat in her intimate relations with the wind and sea.

Once or twice in *Sailing Alone around the World*, Joshua Slocum achieved a similar effect; but in *The Saga of Cimba* this tight focus on the conjunction between hull and wave is a guiding principle of the book, and it yields passage after passage of thrilling writing, as *Cimba*—a frail contraption of wood, brass, canvas, and cordage—confronts the ocean, painted by Maury in every passing mood.

IT IS THE MAGIC of Maury's prose style that raises *The Saga of Cimba* so far above the general run of sea-writing. It's worth glancing here at the drawings that Maury made to illustrate his book, which combine in equal parts a sure-handed economy of line, a fastidious regard for technical detail, and a romantic sense of dramatic occasion. One sees the same combination at work in his writing; but where the drawings are those of a very talented amateur, the writing is that of a master. I think the best clue to its peculiar excellence lies in a remark that Maury makes about his reading at sea. When he finds himself unable to read "literature drab in contrast with the clean, majestic action of the sea," he settles on *Kenilworth*, Sir Walter Scott's lavishly appointed historical novel set in and around the court of Elizabeth I.

Unsatisfied by the writing of his own time—a period of hardboiled reportage, the studied simplicity of Hemingway, and the heyday of the "proletarian novel"—Maury turned to the past for richer fare. *The Saga of Cimba* is peppered with references to writers—Conrad, of course, but also Shakespeare, Melville, Dickens, Stevenson, Rupert Brooke; and one sees how Maury's own writing was shaped by his sea reading, which consisted largely of books that had fallen out of fashion in the 1930s but answered his demand for literature sufficiently "majestic" and "clean" to match the grandeur of the circumstances in which it was being read.

Maury's style is elevated a notch or two above the normal for its time. He favors grammatical tweaks and inversions that are more commonly met in poetry than in prose: "Quickly I heaved at the companion hatch . . . Foot by foot the crawl to windward was carried out . . . Gently she slid over Long Island Sound . . . In the vast gloom the little schooner hurried." This slight literary formality of tone enables Maury to phrase the arresting, high-wire metaphors and similes that are his hallmark: the sun going down in a "ruin of copper"; *Cimba* climbing "a black slide of sea"; a wave curling "our way, a single cap of fluid silver hovering overhead"; the schooner's "spirit laid bare by the sun and shrouded by misty nights of sleeping seas"; "The wind has drawn off beneath the water-painted sky, leaving the sea old, affable, and also painted." This is consciously sumptuous language, but Maury is never guilty of writing purple prose. His most daring flights of figurative writing are also meticulously exact. And they are there on every page. Somehow, from his reading and from his experience, Maury managed to create a style for himself that is uncannily like that of the sea itself, in its fusion of cleanness and majesty.

He was also gifted with an unfailing ear for the cadences of English. If you read him aloud, you hear immediately how each sentence moves to its own meter. When the action speeds up, as it does in the description of the storm off Bermuda in chapters 5 and 6, the tempo quickens to an urgent drumbeat, tempting the reader to turn the pages so fast that the details of the story begin to blur. Never mind. This is a book that can be read a dozen times, and still surprise you with its local splendors.

No one has created a better, more alarmingly convincing storm at sea—not even Conrad in *Typhoon*, or Richard Hughes in *In Hazard*, who are the two leading contenders in the verbal storm-picture department. But it is in the quiet and pensive spells of the voyage that Maury triumphs as a literary stylist. Should you (by any chance) be reading this in a bookstore, wondering whether or not to buy *The Saga of Cimba*, go straight to the bottom of page 112 and read from there to the middle of page 127—Maury's account of "A typical day while running down the south-east trades." Here is an enthralling short story, complete in itself, in which no obvious drama happens, no revelations or discoveries are made, no new port is reached, and yet a whole, busy, complex, and exciting life at sea is conjured out of nothing in less than 2,500 words. The wizardry of the piece is all in the phrasing and the details. Every one of the reader's five senses is kept fully exercised: we see, we hear, we smell, we touch, we taste—we're there on watch, and it is our hand that is on the tiller. I've read several thousands of pages, by dozens of authors, about trade-wind sailing, and I'd happily swap them all for these fifteen.

IF *THE SAGA OF CIMBA* has a single driving theme, it is that in sailing a small boat across the open sea a man may experience something that answers to his own inexhaustible capacity for wonder. Asked why he was undertaking the voyage, Maury claimed that he could not put his reasons into words. "It was like asking a boy why he liked cake, an old man his pipe. We take what we can get." But his writing is itself the perfect answer to the question. The book by no means glosses over the price paid to make the voyage—its toll in death, sickness, frustration, ill-feeling, and the eventual loss of the boat. It justifies that price by placing the reader at the helm of *Cimba*, letting you feel on your own pulse just how it was. Who would not risk life and comfort for such palpable, transfiguring magnificence?

Maury is such a grandly accomplished writer; the sad fact remains that *The Saga of Cimba* is the only book of his that we can read. When it appeared in 1939, it was greeted with a small avalanche of admiring reviews which compared Maury with Anne Lindbergh, Antoine de Saint-Exupéry, Masefield, and—inevitably—Conrad. The *New York Times* reviewer voiced the prevailing response to *Cimba* when he wrote: "There is a spare, taut beauty, a stinging intensity, a fine exhilaration, in this saga of wind and wave." The book was seen as the debut of an exceptional writer from whom much more would be heard.

Within weeks of its publication, Hitler invaded Poland and World War II broke out in Europe. Maury, whose mother was English (his father was American, a direct descendant of the great nineteenth-century circumnavigator and hydrographer Matthew Fontaine Maury, author of *The Physical Geography of the Sea*), enlisted in the British merchant navy, serving as a training officer in Canada. In 1941, after Pearl Harbor and the U.S. entry into the war, he switched to the American merchant service and sailed in convoys across both the Atlantic and Pacific. When the war ended, he took a job with the new Onassis shipping line, captaining decommissioned Liberty ships.

Yet he meant to follow the example of his secret patron saint, and leave the sea for a career in literature. After his marriage in 1948, he quit the Onassis line and set up shop as a writer, working in California on a novel set in New York City and titled *Doomsday Night*. The book went through a number of drafts, under the editorial guidance of Willis Wing, Maury's New York literary agent. The manuscript went back and forth from coast to coast, with revisions piling on revisions, though whether Wing ever actually submitted it to a publisher is unclear. In 1950, with the novel entering its fourth draft (as his wife, Lynn Maury, now remembers), Maury ran into Onassis's New York representative, who persuaded him to make one last sea trip, as captain of a ship bound from New York to Oakland. In Oakland, Maury reluctantly agreed to stay with the ship on its next leg, to the Gulf of Mexico. He remained at sea for the best part of the next thirty years, finally swallowing the anchor in 1978, when he retired to Santa Barbara, California. He tried his hand at writing plays. His family remember the "wonderful" letters that he wrote, datelined from ports around the globe. But *Doomsday Night* is lost. Could it, perhaps, still be found, in a cardboard box in someone's attic or garage?

Richard Maury died in 1998, aged 87. His obituary in the London *Daily Telegraph* was headlined "Author of a minor classic"; but *The Saga of Cimba* is something more than merely minor. Though it is a solitaire diamond, its startling brilliance qualifies it to be remembered as one of the most important books ever to be written about the sea.

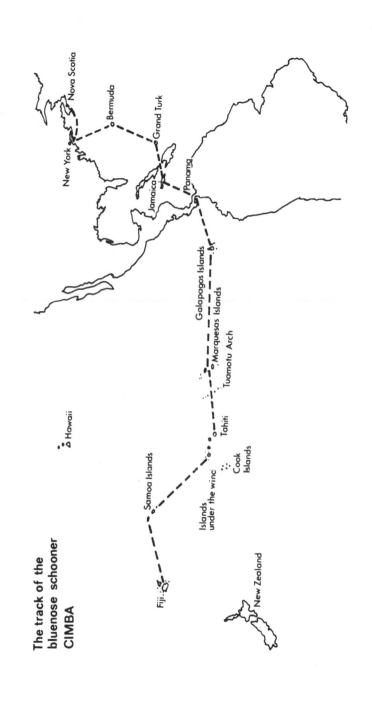

The track of the
bluenose schooner
CIMBA

Nova Scotia
Bermuda
Grand Turk
New York
Jamaica
Panama
Galapagos Islands
Marquesas Islands
Tuamotu Arch
Tahiti
Cook Islands
Islands under the wind
Samoa Islands
Hawaii
Fiji
New Zealand

PREFACE

THIS IS A STORY of adventure, the tale of a cruising schooner at sea, trekking island to island half round the world. To write it has been both painful and pleasant, reviving memories of winds, old sails, faces, and far-away shores; pleasant because of these, but painful also because of disasters, strange, unforeseen, and all too true. The story strives to deal directly with the Sea, the spirit of the schooner, and her harbours, and perhaps to tell, without explaining, of the vision young men behold and cannot explain, and the action that must complement the vision.

Before weighing anchor I wish, even while handicapped by the enforced formality of a preface, to thank with all my heart those of many ports, of many latitudes and longitudes, who stood by the *Cimba*—from Mr William Crosby, of the *Rudder* magazine, New York, whose permission to include portions of an earlier work marks but one more kindness extended, to Mr Alexander Bentley and the sea-lovers of Fiji, and back again to the Indian Point men of Nova Scotia. Some of the *Cimba's* friends —alas, even so soon—are no longer alive, while the names of others, due to pure necessity in the fashioning of this book, will not be found herein. But may I say, from the bottom of my heart, not one shall be forgotten.

Here, then, is the tale, the sea, and the sails of the schooner herself.

R. M.

PREFACE TO THE 1973 EDITION

Since this account of a schooner sailing out her youth in the far seas first appeared in print, the world has moved on. I hope that its reappearance today may convey to new readers something of the flavour and feeling of earlier ocean voyaging and of sailing the South Seas in those splended halcyon years before the last great war: those astoundingly innocent, incredibly glamorous years now gone. Even then one sensed their vulnerability, their poised suspension, like a wave amid shoalwater cresting, alas, only too soon to break.

The *Cimba's* many adventures have themselves become but one with memory. Only the eternals she struggled amidst and toward remain: the power and passion of the sea; the ever-lonely realms of islands; the beckoning planes of lagoons, chopped and windy beyond the reef; and ever the wind, the ocean wind, in rigging and sailcloth and palm trees, itself a memoried echo out of all sea time past. May other and future young seafarers, standing forth into these, find nothing less noble, in their quest for the bright and the brave and the all-remarkable.

November 4th, 1972   Richard Maury

ONE

TOWARDS THE SEA

WE SAW HER first from the top of the cliff. She turned at her chains to every attack of wind, swaying, airy, and buoyant, as though cut of fragile porcelain on the sea below. She was a two-masted schooner, almost as small as they go, almost as stalwart, and, for all the evidence of wood and metal, failing to appear entirely material—an illusion she carried unto the end.

Far down, at the foot of the cliff, came the unmistakable

sound of a dory being hove into water. We began to descend; we were going to board that craft.

Four years before one Vernon Langille, master-builder, had laid the keel of a miniature schooner a few miles up this Nova Scotia coast. He had been closely watched by the people of the fishing village of Indian Point, for the work of Langille, the foremost designer-builder of small ships on the coast, demanded watching. Would the new schooner be a serious contender at the yearly race on St Margaret's Bay? She was small yet neat, with smooth sides lacking so much as half a foot's surface free of curve. Even before being rigged or painted it was evident that she had looks.

But, looks or no looks, after her launching any individuality she may have had in those early days would have been lost amid her sisters, the little inshore fishermen, had it not been for one feature: she was white-painted, the lone white craft in all that black-and-green fleet. A name printed on her tuck should have helped in the matter of identity, but in Nova Scotia small ships are of the hardworking humble, for whom there is little or nothing in a name; so the new schooner became conveniently known as the White 'Un.

Records show that her early life was devoted to retaining, or, rather, developing, an identity. At the close of her first year she appeared on the 'battle-line' of the annual free-for-all on St Margaret's Bay. Her many sisters, in racing trim, were on hand, as were a few craft from the realms of Brass and Varnish, moving swiftly behind the small White 'Un, which saved the day for the Indian Pointers by winning the race. The following season, in a harder struggle, she repeated the feat, and after winning for the third year in succession she became looked upon as one of the smartest craft on the coast. Though still miscalled, her name began to spread.

Just at this point in her career Carrol Huddleston and I, both very young, were meeting in New York to hunt down a small hull that could withstand the seas flowing our imaginations—a hull we could drive to the South Pacific, to islands appearing on little-used charts, perhaps even drive all the way round the world. This scheme had lured Carrol, a civil engineer, out of Central American jungles, and had taken me temporarily from an office in which I held a minor post after returning from a sea of freight steamers, an oil-tanker, and one memorable sailing-ship.

This lure of the sea and a small ship was no light whim; nor was it something formed during listless interludes before fireplaces. Our approach was, rather, cold-blooded and decidedly determined. Regardless of what we *did* find, the quest was not for a life of the sort dreams are made of, and I suppose it might be said that we were seeking a life more vital, or merely for more of life. But at any rate this venture, which Carrol had been driving towards for thirteen years, myself for more than six, remained elusively beyond.

At this point, which we considered an advanced one, the great difficulty lay in obtaining the boat. Nothing we came upon would meet a demanding combination of size, seaworthiness, and price. The last requirement was more important than the first, while the second remained the prime essential of the three. Yet size too was important, that the upkeep would not be exorbitant. Lists of second-hand yachts and large ship's boats were combed in vain. Many an alleged bargain was hunted down, only for it to be discovered that bargains, one and all, were unseaworthy. Three times we felt we had what was wanted, in the end only to be back where we started.

By little more than accident we met George Stadel, a very capable naval architect of Stamford, Connecticut, who told of a wild Nova Scotian fisherman looking for new owners. We were interested. Still, she was far away, and to get to her would mean a voyage in itself. He produced a photograph, at best not much to go by. Finally Carrol remarked, with the unsparing deliberation of a nautical critic, "She's not *bad*."

That night we knew that we were going north, whether to gamble or not. On the following morning I gave up my post at the office, and a day or so later we sailed in the steamer *Arcadia* to slumbering Yarmouth. An all-day journey by rail took us to Mahone Bay, where we struck out on a lonely road through the Lunenburg country, to find at its end the ghost village of Indian Point, the home of the schooner. But she was not there, and only after a search down-coast did we finally come upon her from the top of the cliff. . . . We climbed into the launched dory and pulled in her direction.

Now a strange feeling that we should approach no closer

to the craft came over us: better leave a dream separated
from reality by a good cable's length of vivid water. But the
oars strained at the thole-pins, the dory bit through the sea,
and we were alongside and swinging on board. Once on
deck the feeling disappeared as real wood and canvas put
an end to dreams that for many a day were replaced by action and work.

One by one the sails were hoisted to the blue afternoon,
the cable slipped, and the schooner stood away over St Margaret's Bay. She manoeuvered well, came about quickly for
a long-keeled craft, pointed high for a schooner, and left
astern a clean wake.

The trial trip ending, she was sailed back to Indian Point,
twenty miles away, running down a five-metre racing shell,
leaving it astern in that clean wake of hers.

Carrol remarked that she took to harbour water, handled
herself well, but begged me to remember that she was in no
way ready for deep-sea work, and that until she could be
beached and the underwater lines seen we were almost as
far as ever from our goal.

Accordingly the next day the schooner was pulled out by
a chain of fishing-folk, sweating on a tackle leading to a pin
in the stem-post. The ships of these people, like their arms,
are stout, a point well illustrated when the White 'Un, hard
on her bilge, was heaved bump by bump over a corduroy of
rough logs. Her appearance was sufficiently delicate to start
me looking along those porcelain-like sides for opening

seams. But nothing happened, nothing at all, and I learned that marine railways and cradles were reserved for vessels of fifty feet or more, and that a small ship, if built 'particular,' had no need for such niceties.

The examination ended, and on the evening of September 8, 1933, the White 'Un changed hands, the transaction completed in a quiet, businesslike manner.

The survey of the schooner had shown that her red coppered surfaces blended well with the white, that the slight apple to the bows gave way at the water-line to a fine-cut entrance beneath, that bilges were hard, while the run, noticeably fine and forming the only concave lines, extended an unusual distance forward. What we had seen was the form of a well-knit model, small, slight, strong, embodying, besides the stout science of boat-building, something more rare—the art that had taken a bundle of wood and tubs of metal fasteners to create an object attaining poise, balance, and, yes, something of beauty—the simple beauty of utility; no other.

It was incredible that Vernon Langille had designed the White 'Un without so much as drawing a line on paper, or even whittling a model for a pattern. He had merely tacked together eight moulds, or life-sized cross-sections, gauging them, one after another, by eye, before immediately starting to build.

But now just what had been acquired for the considerable task ahead? A schooner of barely five tons, thirty-five feet overall, twenty-six at the waterline, and only three feet a few inches in draught; a little harbour schooner, a stranger to ocean weather, a craft that save for a small cuddy forward was entirely open, with an unprotected fishing-well running her length to hold the eight hundred pounds of stone ballast. There was no bowsprit. Two frail masts raked unconvincingly into the air, stayed but lightly against the winds of land-bounded waters. As yet she was a long way from the sea.

The hull—the main consideration—had an easy grace to it, a sweep of elliptical deck-lines swelling to extreme beam, and there immediately falling away. There was a decided dip to the sheer, typical of the true fisherman, a spoon bow, and a fisherman counter—often called a towboat stern.

Work was commenced. Masts and rigging were sent down, the cuddy ripped out, and a pair of cabins built over the hold; atop these hand-rails were fastened. A one-ton shoe of iron was bolted to the keel and held between false pieces, hardwood members that, carrying out the new line, increased the draught. New masts of spruce were stepped, stayed with ⅜-inch galvanized wire, and secured with dead-eyes and lanyards.

A word about the below. The newly built main cabin commenced at the break of the foremast, and terminated at the mainmast. The after-cabin was smaller, separated from the main by an amidships bulkhead, outside by a well-deck. The main cabin was scored to take three large portholes and one small one. A companionway was built to starboard, while simple bins, protruding from the skin, formed the back of two coffin-like bunks, six feet long and eighteen inches wide. Forward of these, opposite and over the fisherman stove, shelving was fixed. Provisions and equipment would be stored in the bins under the bunks, with the bulk put into the after-cabin, while in the eyes (opening directly on to the main cabin) another shelf would serve for the stowing of sail-cloth and ground tackle. The after-cabin could be entered from a hatch to port, and had only one port-light. Here an ancient 8-horse, two-cylinder make-and-break engine rested below a pair of tanks, which together held twenty-five gallons of fuel. Forward of the engine the two water-tanks, heavy, soldered, riveted, each holding thirty gallons, were, for safety as well as to discourage waste, equipped with the smallest of bronze spigots. Aft a compass swung in a binnacle built under a deadlight on the cabin-top.

On deck, immediately abaft the after-cabin, was the steering-well, small and snug, its either side holding small lockers, one for lamps, loglines, leadlines, the other for equipment needed in emergencies—strops, reef earings, sail gaskets, small stuff, a marline-spike, an extra knife, a fog-horn. Abaft the steering-well was the watertight door of the lazarette, a place set aside to hold such bosun's stores as paint and spare halyards. To ensure dryness the schooner was allowed no forepeak hatch, no skylights. Cabin-tops and decks, as is customary in small Nova Scotians, were left uncorked, their smooth, utterly flawless surfaces appearing to be canvased.

A few statistics:

Length, over all	35 ft. 3 in.
Length, water-line	26 ft.
Beam	9 ft. 6 in.
Depth (aft)	5 ft.
Head-room	4 ft. 8 in.

Framing: Steam-bent, on 8-in. centres; of oak.

Planking: 1¼-in. red pine below water, white above.

Keel, stem-piece, stern-piece, mast partners, and natural knees of oak.

Fittings: By local blockmakers and smithies.

Sail-plan: Cut by sailmaker of the schooner *Blue-nose*. A fisherman's working rig—gaff-rigged mainsail and foresail; one jib.

A month later the schooner was ready to leave the ways. The cabins were painted white, trimmed grey, while outside the green-and-white fishing colours of the hull were brightened up. Then at last she was launched.

Before this came about her real name had been discovered under the steep slope of the counter—the inspiring one of *Wassoc*! It would not do at all. But Vernon Langille, following a custom of using the same name-board for each new ship, ripped it off, leaving the White 'Un nameless. In due course it was replaced by one in honour of a nearly forgotten

Aberdeen merchant ship, one of the smaller, lesser-known wool-clippers, yet one of the noblest, under whose white spear of jib boom a lion rampant had snarled, leaping from a bow on which was painted the short, lionlike name of Cimba. And the White 'Un had received her name!

Warren Heisler was to make the passage to America with us. From the first this large, comely, rather romantic soul, the supreme figure of Indian Point, had been our staunch friend. Although scarcely thirty, it was legend that on the Banks there was no better doryman than Warren, and on the shore no one more cool-headed or dependable. He had been 'away,' and his knowledge of the sea and of men was indisputable.

Finally came the night when all was ready. As we awaited Warren and his gear before turning in Carrol and I stood in the moonlight watching the *Cimba* swaying in her new strength. She was eager to be off, she who had been mothered in quiet harbours, who was young, untried. Would she live to swing some day to other winds in other harbours, far down in the enchanted South Oceans? Would she? Far across from Heisler's Island, over the gleaming bay, came the answering night wind: "Go on! . . . Go on! . . . "

$\mathcal{TWO}$

THE GALE AND THE LEE SHORE

THE FIRST sailing day was a bright one. At eleven o'clock canvas was hoisted, a conch shell sounded a farewell, and the schooner glided towards the intricate channels leading to the sea. In mid-harbour she faltered for wind, moved once again, fetched channel, slid over it, and Indian Point was seen no more.

For hours we worked seaward, and then, near sunset, the schooner felt her first ground swells. Land still guarded her, but now over the bows lay a line of rolling ocean, shining

and cold. The running engine tried to drive the bows under, but the forward sections resisted, passing seas harmlessly
over shoulder, sending spray into our intent faces.

While we lacked sea-room a bottle of Demerara, the gift
of a concerned friend, was brought on deck, broached, and
a toast drunk to the success of the venture. This one time
liquor was permitted on board remains clear in mind, the
young three of us, wet with spray, tippling a bottle, while the
Cimba smashed a way to sea—a dark waste on which the
sunset died, over which winds from the south-east came to
redden our wetted faces.

Two miles off the engine was stopped, sails were broken
out, and a course was shaped for Cape Sable, eighty miles
away, the last land to be picked up before the Cape Cod
Canal entrance, lying on our way to Stamford, on Long
Island Sound.

The end of the dusk revealed the small form of the
schooner staggering under a loom of canvas that even as I
watched seemed to increase in size with the coming of darkness; and there came the sober conviction that beneath us
lunged a frail craft of which we were asking a great deal. Sea
and darkness closed in; winds ran the quarter as the delicate curve of bow thundered in the night and the low sides
sheared the chop rising above them. Astern a corkscrew of
wake flashed, one long, ever-rolling path over a constant rise
and fall of unseen waves. Now and then on the coast to starboard clusters of lights were seen burning, unwavering, still,

appearing remote and lost in space, like visions of ghost villages never again to be visited.

The first four-hour watch was mine. Part of it was spent in the rapid reeling-off of knots, part with the schooner seemingly lost, dissolved away in seawater and a blackness that left only the feel of her sway, the feel of the hard oak tiller, the foot-braces of the steering-well. Warren relieved me for the graveyard watch, while Carrol, in the four-to-eight, brought us abeam Cape Sable, to take departure for Cape Cod, two hundred and twenty miles across the Gulf of Maine.

Daylight, and the *Cimba* was no more the uninitiated of the evening past, no more a stranger to the scheme of the sea. The sun was lost in cloud, the wind fell, and watch followed watch with the schooner slow-moving over leaden levels. All day she heaved restlessly, while the sun circled the sky, unseen until falling, a ruin of copper, into dark horizon mist. A cold night swept up the skylines, bringing no change.

Next day schooner and ocean were active again as a sharp north-easter started seas that raced a scud of cold, westing cloud. Thunder sounded, a heavy barrage of rain struck decks, and the *Cimba* leaped to action, running hour after hour with straining sheets.

At three we were ready to shorten sail. Carrol was at the helm, Warren and I stood by the halyards, keeping lookout through the rain.

Suddenly Warren shouted, "There's one of those no-good pirates now! To port, there! Come in on him, Carrol!"

Heading was altered until the bows pointed on a steam trawler a quarter of a mile off.

A race started. The steamer, on a course parallel to ours, was running with the seas for all she was worth. But the White 'Un ran faster, lunging off the lips of waves as though built for that one purpose. Soon the symbol of some large corporation painted on the stack of the steamer was plainly seen. The schooner flew through the trawler's smoke, came so close abeam that her new name could be read from the stranger, then flashed ahead. What could the Gloucester skipper have thought on seeing a twenty-six-foot water-liner go by him in a blow? He must have been making his nine knots. Then, too, what were his reactions on seeing a ship's mop mastheaded to the schooner by the ever thorough Warren? Did he grasp the significance of the insult? We were of the opinion that he did, that it was he himself who came out of the wheelhouse to shake a fist. We were also of the opinion that he was smiling, and that the shaken fist only indicated an observation of all things traditional.

Slowly the trawler dropped out of sight. The wind held long after the sun went, and the *Cimba* raced through another night, raised Cape Cod, and was immediately hove-to. In the morning sail was set to a heavy wind, and we felt through rain and fog for Sandwich and the entrance to the Canal. Visibility was lost; an onshore wind grew stronger. Land appeared, undefined, uncertain, and then, after debating quickly, we prudently came about and set to sea in a rising storm.

"A good move, and just in time!" sang out Warren.

Under double reefs we screwed the *Cimba* to windward, wondering, as the tophamper leaned to the blow, how a one-ton keel and a few hundred pounds of ballast could keep her upright. It seemed brutal to jam that thin body into the steep, knotted-up seas so green and cut with windwash. It had to be done. A lee shore was uncomfortably by, the engine irrevocably dead. The blow came in heavy gusts, causing the schooner to stagger, to bury lee sides to the cabin-tops, to quiver. She would lock herself under a roller, then claw for the cap, straining, fighting back, and up, and forward.

Through morning and into afternoon this went on, this groping a way to sea. We kept to the deck, where the actions and the angles of the craft made us hold on with both hands. Even Warren, the perfect small-boatman, found the going difficult that day. Carrol was sick, the icy rain beating into his face; and yet he, right from the tropics, insisted on standing his full wheel trick, from noon to four. In vain Warren and I tried to take the tiller from him: he had always a stubborn look for us, a ghastly smile for the drive of rain.

Before his watch was over I opened the hatch and went below to look at the chart. Jumping down, I slammed-to the hatch as a wall of water slid over the rail. The cabin, as they sometimes say, was a hurrah's nest. Neatly lined shelves had been emptied by the diving schooner. Equipment, clothes, blankets, had been flung on to the floor-boards, to toss to and fro in small seas of their own. The warmth of the coal stove had been lost by sea-water flooding the Charlie Noble—that object sometimes called a stovepipe. Dream ship?

Well, scarcely that day, although, as one old philosopher said, "Ships is only dreams before and after you've sailed 'em."

No sooner had I found the chart than I began feeling slightly dizzy. It seemed as though the schooner was labouring more than ever, that the cabin was growing unusually dark. For the first time I became aware of a heavy, a rather sweet, odour. Then it struck me that gas from a leaking tank in the after-cabin was seeping forward in the bilges, that the cabin was partially filled with it. Quickly I heaved at the companion hatch. It was wet, new, and stiff, and would not give. I called out to Warren. There was no answer. I called again, but still no answer came. Too much wind! Going to a port-light, I worked on a securely fastened screw. By now my fingers had lost feeling, and only my eyes testified that they were working. There was the shock of a wave on the weather side, the cabin tilted, and the *Cimba* slipped off a sea. She fell, and I fell with her, landing on the dunnage of the floorboards. The cabin seemed much darker as I got to my feet and braced myself against the bulkhead, feeling for the screw. After a final turn I swung the rim open and, putting forth my head, called out. Sounds of savage kicking on the companion followed. It gave with a crash, and down jumped Warren, who without a word heaved me to the hatch, where I climbed into the rain to see Carrol, still at the helm, eyeing me with concern. And there on deck the roaring wind, the cold rains and spray, soon revived me.

Foot by foot the crawl to windward was carried out. Afternoon passed into night, and still it went on. At nine, when thirty miles off, wind and sea overpowered us, until we could sail no more. After shortening down to a foresail the helm was lashed alee, and, following the customary procedure, we went below. The fuel leak had been stopped, the bilges cleaned, the cabin ventilated, and, after many attempts, a fire was kindled in the stove. Beside its glowing body we had a much-needed meal of codfish and tea. Talk followed. Carrol, now well after facing the weather all day, told of tropical adventures, his quiet voice contrasting with the storm sliding over the cabin-top. Warren matched them with a wild, an incredible, story of the wild, incredible sea. The lantern light swung rapid shadows across their faces as I, the quiet listener, broke silence only to urge them on.

In a little while the talk broke up. Again we were considering the weather and computing the drift on to the Cape. Shortly afterwards a look-out was posted. All was well at midnight, at one, at two. At three o'clock Carrol and I heard Warren's voice hailing from on deck. We hurried up, finding the night dark, holding a smashing wind—and breakers three hundred yards to leeward!

So the worst had happened! The engine was dead, and a wind we thought too strong to sail against was driving us ashore. It had taken us unexpectedly, but not to find us unprepared. The proper action had been determined beforehand—a simple one, the only one left—merely that of clapping on more sail and trusting that the schooner could live under it and beat for sea.

Carrol and Warren swayed up the big mainsail, while I, getting forward, hoisted the saturated jib. The *Cimba's* canvas was never handled more efficiently; even so, by the time the sails were in the wind the craft was less than a hundred yards off-shoal. She leaned sharply as the gale felt of her cloth; then yawed when a wave, picking her up, swept her towards the reef. There was a loud explosion of close-by water battering unseen rock. In the backflow of the wave the *Cimba* began to sail, with lee housing under and the weather rail fencing off a furious chop.

I found a straining backstay in the dark, clung to it, and looked over the bows. We were taking the wind to port, with Carrol again at the helm, pinching the craft into it on a tack no better than parallel with the surf. She dipped deep in a trough, came up, and I saw breakers dead ahead. We had to come about immediately. Carrol let her fall towards the surf, gained headway, and put the helm down. I worked forward with Warren, forcing the jib aback. She spun on her keel, and in an increased noise of wind-mad canvas came over, fell rigidly in a trough, and lay as though never to rise. Then, in the sweep of a sea that edged her towards shoal, she righted herself, took a full blast of wind, and began to sail.

For three hours she pitched to a stiff sea, clawing off, putting the breakers astern. She actually sailed into the gale, to windward, hammering, labouring, drenching her sails every foot of the way.

At dawn it moderated. The sun came into a blue sky, and we ran for Sandwich under full press, with blankets and clothes strung to the lifelines, drying in the cool autumn wind. At seven we sighted a fleet of steam trawlers, which even as we bore down found the seas still too high and put back for shore. The schooner was off Sandwich at eight, trying to sail into the narrow entrance against a land wind. The engine wouldn't start, and we could not pinch a way into the channel. As no flag could be found we signalled for a tow with a pair of pyjamas triced in the fore-rigging. A motor-sailer came out and towed us over the short distance to the jetty, where Captain I. L. Hammond, of the Coast Guard, on seeing the state of affairs below, insisted that we breakfast at the station.

And there we heard that after being sighted heading to sea the previous morning we had been given up for lost. Within a few miles of us a three-funnel liner had been hove-to for thirty-six hours, and not far away the finest three-master out of Lunenburg had foundered with all hands while the *Cimba* strove through her first test.

Without making use of the station's sleeping quarters, generously offered by Captain Hammond, we set to work to overhaul the engine, and, this completed, headed for our destination on Long Island Sound.

Two nights later, while nearing Stamford, the watch below came on deck to stand by the helmsman. The night was dark, the sea quiet, the schooner echoing our voices.

"We worked well together in that blow," said one.

"Yes; no shouting. I don't think anyone gave an order."

"It's just as well they didn't. If a man doesn't know how

to handle himself without being told in a craft this size he's better off at home. We—well, we came through fairly well."

"We were lucky too," remarked Carrol, with a good deal of truth.

Then Warren, agreeing, told of a time when he had been picked up after having been lost in a dory on the Grand Banks.

"And that was luck too," he laughed, "except I reckon there isn't any luck on the old sea—only a lot of destiny."

The topic changed to the real, the unquestionable, hero of all these small-boat journeys—to the craft herself.

Gently she slid over Long Island Sound. In the east burned some stars, the only lights in a huge shadowed sky. The two philosophers mused on, Warren with his big head propped on his knees, Carrol gazing into the unwavering glow of the binnacle. . . . Lift . . . lift . . . fall . . . She moved like a dark bird against the few stars.

Early on the 15th of October the *Cimba* entered the dreary waters of Stamford Harbour, the smallest of a fleet of thirteen to make the Nova Scotian passage, bettering the time for the run by a day and a half. With clacking sheets she sailed a narrowing shore, an unpretentious, rather humble white schooner, as likely as not unnoticed amid the sleek forms of anchored yachts. Her foresail was lowered, and, turning off-channel, she entered a little creek, there to be outfitted for the distant South Seas.

THREE

DEPARTURE

THE OCEAN routes immediately ahead of the *Cimba*: New York to Bermuda, Bermuda to Caribbean ports, to the Panama Canal, where the attack on the Pacific would commence.

A great deal was done before leaving Stamford for New York, the port of departure. On the afterdeck a gallows frame was set up to take the weight of the main boom. A small hatch, secured from below, was cut on the main cabin-top, giving more light and ventilation than a skylight, while offering a flat surface on deck. A new arc of oak, a tiller comb, was fitted on the after-deck immediately under a straight tiller, so equipped with a tooth that it could be jammed at any angle into notches on the comb. To obtain greater leverage on the helm a short length of oak with a brass flange that could be shipped or unshipped at short notice was made to socket round the tiller-end. A tarpaulined object, eight feet by two feet, and but a few inches high, was secured to the cabin trunk. This was the collapsible tender. The fore-rigging was rattled down, and the four stranded lanyards setting up the stays were replaced by ones of Italian hemp. Below the stone ballast was taken out, and a thousand pounds of iron battened to the bilges. Another berth was rigged in the main cabin, a canvas one, which could be rolled away against the skin. The engine was taken down, overhauled, and set up again. The cabins were painted; the hull was painted.

Then stores and equipment—an unending, miscellaneous list of them—were taken aboard: stock-anchors and sea-anchors, international signal flags, cabin lamps, anchor lights, sailmaker's stores (spare canvas, roping, sail-twine); a boatswain's chair, spare blocks, a watch tackle, a gun tackle; paint, white lead, tar, oakum; a good sextant, a well-rated chronometer, a pair of binoculars, parallel rules, pilot-books, light-lists, and a vast collection of charts; a 30.30 Winchester repeater; medicines, chosen for the trip by Dr Slaughter, of Darien, and a medical kit, carefully packed by Carrol's sister, Dr Jean Huddleston, through thick and thin the schooner's most loyal friend. Donations followed: the generous gifts of a weather coat for the man at the helm, a very accurate U.S. Navy star-guide, a .38 revolver, a 12-gauge shotgun, and a

Genoa jib from an 'R' boat, recut to make an excellent fisherman staysail.

In spite of this large amount of equipment an air of strict, almost puritanical simplicity was retained about the craft. And if simplicity ruled on deck, where the three modest working, sails, all inboard, were free of topping-lifts and lazy lacks, then also it ruled below. As previously mentioned, the after-cabin was devoted to the engine, tanks, and bulk stores. The main had its bunks, its well-filled lockers, a stove; no more. On the port bulkhead was a picture of the original *Cimba,* presented by Frank Jaeger, sailing-ship historian, and, like Alfred Cook, another of the *Cimba*'s friends, a builder of fine ship models. On the starboard bulkhead, opposite the Scottish *Cimba,* was a chromo of Miss Elissa Landi, the two pictures representing the ever-full yet divided heart of the sailor.

The narrow bunks had neither springs nor yacht mattresses. The mouths of two gunny-sacks filled with straw and bed-grass were laced together with sail-twine to replace mattresses, which, once wet, soon mildew. These donkey's breakfasts, as they were once called, could easily be replaced by new ones at the end of every trip. Springs rust, break, and are less than luxuries at sea, so the bunks had slats of oak.

If simplicity was an aim, then so also was safety. Overhead in the cabin a small ship's bell was fixed with a toggled lanyard running from its clapper through the bulkheads to the steering-well. Signals were arranged for the helmsman: one bell, change of watch; two, handle sail; three or more, emergency, hands on deck.

It was decided that Carrol should do the offshore navigating, the piloting to remain a mutual burden. The decision was prompted by his aptitude for the science, by his precision and skill in mathematical realms; these, rather than a technical background, or in spite of it, were the deciding factors, along with the old proverb that too many cooks spoil the broth.

This became definitely settled when I was told point-blank that I had journalistic tendencies, and that an account of the cruise of the *Cimba* was to appear each month in the *Rudder* magazine. So was it planned that in the precious moments between standing watch and sleeping one would work in figures, the other in words.

Already we knew something of what the voyage would demand. Unless gravely mistaken we were in for no drifting-match to the South Seas. The very first run would likely take our measure, for already winter was hurrying on its way, and the Gulf Stream and Hatteras would surely be acting up. No, we looked forward to a lively, full-hearted affair on roaring water, spent on the eager deck, within the diving cuddy of a highly tempered craft—a small craft, carrying within her insignificant body a soul as stormy as the winds of her Nova Scotia. And through all this we caught the dim form of Adventure, as only youth may sight it undismayed.

* * *

ON THE 26th of October our trio was broken when Warren, bound for Stamford in one of the *Cimba*'s sisters, was
swept overboard and drowned in the North Atlantic. On the
5th of November, a few days before the start, Carrol was
lost while tending the *Cimba* alone in the driving sleet in the
darkness of Stamford Harbour. So did they go, unto the end
lovers and comrades of the Sea; and they went bravely, without fear, like brother-adventurers slipping off together towards the Great Sea of their hearts.

FOUR

WINTER, NORTH ATLANTIC

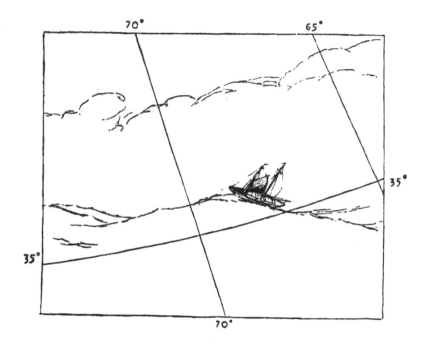

AUTUMN AGED into winter, and the cold reaches of Stamford Creek became more sullen than ever. Shipyards lost their hypnotic appeal, were presently abandoned, and work on the schooner became less and less interrupted. Occasionally a friend bundled in an overcoat braved the wind to persuade me from the venture; but only occasionally. Each day found the *Cimba* more prepared for flight, less tender, stiffer, lower in the water. Finally, on a winter's evening when the Sound was deserted, the last yacht hauled out, all was ready.

Sailing day! Day of days in the life of every craft—that momentous time when one sees with uncertain eyes the dream ready to move, to sail out with the flood to some awaiting test. From plans and books, hope and work, came this, the *Cimba's* sailing day. And now it was of little use for anyone to point out that no craft so small had weathered the Gulf Stream on a winter voyage to Bermuda. The schooner was shipshape, well-found; every conceivable precaution had been taken. For the rest, she would sail to course and schedule as we had planned.

"Dombey" Russell Dickinson, apprenticed in sail, young steamship officer, skeleton skipper of a tied-up windjammer, now to take his chances with a wandering Bluenoser, shared this feeling as we lay at Pier 6, New York City, awaiting the tide. Tall and rangy, of my own age—twenty-three—gifted with a deep topsail-yard voice, capable in a seaway, affable ashore, he had joined forces in that last moment.

The *Cimba* floated small and white under the skyscrapers, lying deep in the water, with little more than a foot of freeboard amidships. But, deep-laden or not, after stowing a hundred books in the forepeak I went ashore, to see an appreciable change in her trim. A group of photographers and reporters stood on the wharf, fascinated by the slim hull, the short masts.

Up the Bay boomed the wind, driving clouds that frowned upon the skyscrapers. I glanced at the heights of stone, bleak, sharp-edged, already greying, shadow on shadow on top of shadow, soon to be hull-down, to be lost track of, forgotten. We drift away from things; sometimes we sail away. . . . It was time to leave, to look our last at the New World, before facing the ageless sea. I fumbled while taking in a spring-line, and with pain in my throat knew again the sadness of parting.

The *Cimba*'s red-and-black house flag whipped taut in the cold wind. There was a great deal of noise from the yellow waves of the Bay, and whistles screamed through the greyness, ghost calling ghost; a rolling Pennsylvania Railroad tug cut close to our quarter. A big Cunarder passed, with tears of rust streaked from her hawse-pipes; a Christmas-painted tanker pushed out to sea; at the Narrows the lonely white form of the *Tusitala* loomed before us, the spears of her yellow yards stabbing the driven wrack. Reverently we dipped the new ensign and headed on. The wind swung into the south-east, increased, and in a wild fire of sunset we came to anchor off Atlantic Highlands to await our chance.

At noon on the last day of November 1933 we secured everything movable on deck, set up lifelines, and after swinging ship for compass deviation took departure off Sandy Hook. Soon the American coast was below the horizon.

As a west wind came off crisp cloud-banks it seemed as though the schooner swayed over-eagerly, that she ran

south-east impetuously, savagely. As yet she was not labouring, but nevertheless we were tempted to take in sail. The elements, and especially the sea, demand the respect of the
conservative side of one's nature. And yet the same sea tends
to draw out any duality in a voyager's nature, to bring forth
his defiant, his carrying-on side, so that his life is one of constant conflict between these two opposing, contradictory
impulses. We clung to our sail as on the starboard beam a
great bloodstained light lowered, grew dim. The wind dried
the blood. They were gone—sunset and our first day! And
sparks like fireflies sailed from the Charlie Noble.

I took the eight-to-twelve wheel (as we often referred to
the helm), and saw the moon come up, baring everything
about, even the reef-points lifting in the gusts. Finely sculp-
tured seas, pale, like the waves in a dream, built up, staggered, shattered, and built up again. A thin way of moonlight
swept across-ocean to the horizon; the *Cimba* sprang through
it, sea to sea, her paintwork alive with shifting shadow, her
rigging moaning, her white hull cutting a shining, running
groove. By and by the moon misted; the sea blackened,
swung less, and staggered more; the west wind tightened.

At midnight a star-fix told that in the last twelve hours the
Cimba had run down 101 miles, averaging 8.4 knots over this
period. She was making better than 9 when I went below,
quite certain that she was in for a dusting.

After hot coffee I lay on the bunk and listened to the
water singing past the hull, then for any sound of straining

timber. There was none. This deceiving craft, running wild with a heavy load, was doing so without a sound, without a creak. But as I listened I heard the wind muffle down, then come on with greater strength. I raised myself for Dombey's signal. It did not come. Turning low the lamp, so that my eyes would be prepared for the darkness, I lay back in the bunk. Again the wind dropped, and again it returned, high and wild, this time with a shriek—a very loud one. And there was the signal!

I was on deck. There was no moon now, and ice could be smelt in the wind. Far to the northward where the sky should have been was a great darkness. The deck was careening, and the time for being conservative was at hand. Then everything seemed to go wrong. As we worked the canvas the foresail jibbed, the main gaff jammed almost simultaneously, and somehow the jib freed itself of the sheets. One moment the schooner had shown smooth sails, the next fouled cloth, flogging, shaking the very masts. The western darkness spread, and a squall, rain-charged, drove up with big seas.

We had to work quickly, by feeling alone—feeling of ropes, canvas, and blocks, frequently saving ourselves from heavy lunges by grappling to hand-rails or a lifeline. The foresail was handled, and after some difficulty the jib, its club swinging dangerously in the dark. Climbing the mast, we brought our weight to bear upon the hoops of the mainsail. The jammed gaff gave, came running down, and we, together with the sail, fell to deck. The gear was quickly lashed with gaskets, a storm trysail was set, and a conical-type sea-anchor laid out over the bows.

Wet through and short of breath, we had time, while waiting for the coffee to warm in the cabin, to think over this incident. A critical moment had found us completely taken aback. Little more than twelve hours out on a cruise to last years we had barely escaped severe punishment. Well, it wouldn't happen again. We were so sure!

For twenty-two hours we were held weatherbound. The sea-anchor lasted six, before being strained out of all recognition, stripped of its canvas, its steel frame bent backward, its oil-tin battered and emptied. A close-reefed foresail was run up, and we lay hove-to until sails were set again. For part of one day the *Cimba* rode large hills of sea, lost amid their ever-wandering bodies, and then, quite suddenly, near night, her headway ceased.

I was at the useless helm; Dombey leaned carelessly against the starboard shrouds. We were studying the weather with such confidence, with a great deal of self-assurance. There would be no change for hours! Just then, without warning, without so much as a stirring of windward water, a broadside of wind struck the idle sails. The craft, lacking headway, was pinned on her beam. Over she went, throwing Dombey into the belly of the main. He reached deck in time to pay off the foresheet as I slammed the tiller alee. The careening ceased, there was a flush of white water on deck, and the craft lifted her shoulder, righted, and began to sail. The wind left as abruptly as it had come, and although we stood ready for any further attacks the isolated gust slanting steeply from high altitudes was not repeated.

In the night it began to blow once more. The craft lay down to it, throwing a bow wave and lifting red-and-green spray past her side-lights. Rain fell. At twelve a passenger liner was sighted closing in on the port quarter. Having had no sights, and being blown off-course, we decided to ask a position of the stranger, a custom almost as old as sailing. When she was half a mile off—she would come no nearer—we played a flashlight on our mainsail and signalled for position in international code. A pause. Then over the ocean a large searchlight cut the rain to blink the word 'latitude.' Another pause. So far so good. A play of light followed, so rapid that the dots were indistinguishable from the dashes. We blinked, "Repeat." No reply came. Again our sail was lit with the signal. But the liner's searchlight died out, and she was away, disappearing over the sea, shrouded in rain, dipping her long-rowed lights to the blustering darkness. We identified her as a South America-bound vessel, sailing under our own flag, and declared that her action would be reported. Of course, it never was, as we, forgetting the incident, recalled only the moral: the sea, the isolating sea, confines one to one's own resources.

Shortly afterwards we were caught in a south-wester. Steep mounds closed about the hull; a hard wind pressed into the tophamper. Desperately we fought to retain headway, and for three wet hours succeeded, before heaving to.

In nautical phraseology when a vessel drops to leeward

with the drift of large waves it is sometimes said that she is so driven by the scend of the sea. On December 4th, upon once more getting under way, we estimated this scend to have carried us a good hundred miles to the north and east of our course. Days were passing, and we were getting nowhere. Our charge must be hard-sailed back to course; and with this in mind Dombey and I began a determined drive to the southward. At noon of the 4th the sails were set. Above them long cloud formations, unwinding from the invisible to windward, smoked the sky; waves shone with a dull metallic gleam, their bellies rolling lava-like, their tops yellowish and blunted. And there was no sun; only mysterious fringes of light shining on the winded edges of clouds. In the vast gloom the little schooner hurried, thrown from sea to sea, pressed down by gust upon gust, a wild fisherman wetting her decks as she reeled off eight and a half knots. An hour passed with all going well; another, and then we were close-hauled, no longer making course, but looking for trouble from the west. For a moment there had been a narrow arch to windward, blue and appearing out of place on the dismal seascape. It had vanished, and as it did all at once the weather sky collapsed, the lights in the clouds were extinguished, and the sea became as black as pitch. Great drifts of vertical wash, suspended for miles across the south horizon, bore down. There was a rustle of wind-eddies on the rolling water. I looked at Dombey, indistinct in the gloom. He glanced at me uneasily. We said nothing, saw to it that halyards were clear, and waited. A silence; then the impact of rain and wind, the schooner tearing to windward, into it, her sails tense, tight against the grey, flying clouds. Her hull gleamed naked in the black seas, the bilges gripped defiantly, and the bows lifted over broken water. How long she would have fought is hard to say. The heroic impulse of a little ship is great. But ten minutes later, hard put to it by the blow, Dombey and I went on the defensive, snugged down, and heaved to in a fifty-mile wind.

The gale swung the compass; then roared out of the north-east for thirty-three hours. When it eased the craft, having sailed only three hours of the past sixty-two, was again driven south for an hour, before being overwhelmed by black squalls and again hove to. By now she was well out in the current of the Gulf Stream, which, opposing a north-easter, stacked the seas in up-and-down formations. In the night the lunge of waves became more powerful, forcing us on deck to make a jury sea-anchor out of a spar and a spare sail weighted with fifty pounds of ballast. The work was done in pouring rain and, the flashlight having become water-soaked, complete darkness. After we had rigged a bridle to the spar the jury anchor was paid out with fifty fathoms of new three-inch manilla. It served well, holding the bows into the wind until it blew a whole gale at 1 A.M. Heavier seas were forced up, the chocks in the bows cut through the cable, parcelled though it was, and both line and gear were lost.

Storm oil was needed badly. Our supply was used up. As a last resort we passed a lanyard about a tin of Stockholm tar, punctured it, eased it over the weather bow, and found to our surprise that it worked. An hour went by, and then a particularly steep sea picked the tin up, hurling it on deck with sufficient force to broach it, daubing the schooner fore and aft, and making the deck more treacherous than ever. Daylight showed a strange-looking black-and-white schooner lying up to a gale with a tar-stained sail.

A siege of heavy weather set in, a siege that held through night and day. Once the port-side light, fastened to its board six feet above the deck, was swept away by seas. Two nights later the starboard one went. Much of the time was passed in our little dugout of a cabin, bracing ourselves to every dip and lunge of the hull, to every pitch the schooner made, as from outside came the uninterrupted sobbing, the suck of heavy weather. Only once in a period of ninety-six hours was any sailing done, when under reduced canvas we drove, pounded, some miles southward. Finally a thermometer hove overside told us that we were south of the Gulf Stream; there were a few hours of sailing before we were again riding out a gale.

Very slowly we closed in on Bermuda, searching for the small islands over dark seas, carrying all possible sail. Two weeks had passed; the Gulf Stream had set us one way, the weather another, until our position was extremely dubious. But one day a blue sky broke above us, and we lay becalmed on an equally blue sea not far from Bermuda. Dombey and I held to the deck, along with wet blankets strung to the lifelines. The quieted shapes of canvas dried in the sun, and the Nova Scotiaman, unused to deep-water seas of blue, scarcely moved beneath us. At three in the afternoon a swell rolled up from the south, and presently a breath of air, warm and salty, touched the sails. I heard Dombey's voice from out of the calm, "Wind to-night."

I put my hand lazily overside. A small fish, a cow pilot, nibbled at it. Now the stir of wind could be felt more distinctly. The sea, even as we watched, turned a darker hue.

"It's here," I said.

"On a bowline though."

Our voices sounded loud amid the quiet. The main sheet cracked taut.

The calm was almost over, as bright wind-clouds crayoned above the skylines indicated. By sundown we were sailing in light breezes, only hoping that they would hold through the night. If they held Bermuda might be raised in the morning. But as it happened they did more than that. Westing until we were close-hauled, they came head-on, blew up! At midnight the schooner was struggling with a starboard tack; at three running a high offing with enthusiasm, with wild ship-like sounds, as determined as her crew in the fight for landfall. The graveyard watch ended, and soon afterwards came the familiar thud of broken seas, the loom of sliding clouds, black, rolling like smoke as they covered the stars. Then in a cry of wind sounding through darkness, horizon to horizon, the craft was once more hove to.

FIVE

THE CAPSIZING

A SCHOONER is usually hove to by securing the helm alee and furling all cloth but the foresail. Once hove to she should, unattended, creep to windward with the foresail, until the rudder has pinched the sail so close into wind that headway becomes lost, and, the vessel falling off, the foresail fills, the manoeuvre being repeated. This counterbalancing of sail and rudder, depending on the force of the wind-sea, should keep the vessel working slowly to windward, holding her own or else falling gradually to leeward.

The *Cimba*, usually a good heavy-weather craft, did not heave to especially well on the night after the calm. The seas were higher than they had been, and neither Dombey nor I could get her lying comfortably amid them. Either she would yaw widely or else pitch into the eye of the wind until we thought her rocking masts would snap their stays. And the fault was not hers, but very much my own. When the draught had been increased in Nova Scotia I was the one who felt that the small original rudder should be kept, that a larger one might part in a seaway. Under ordinary conditions the rudder worked well, but now, with waves high enough partially to blanket sail and lessen headway, it lacked sufficient surface to force the hull to the wind.

We tried righting this with more headway to give greater rudder action, taking the close reef out of the foresail and running it up single-reefed. But the sail, overpowering the rudder, sheared the schooner broadside to the first big sea. She slid into a trough. The double reef was quickly put back and a storm trysail set to the main, a combination successful once or twice before, but now throwing us into the eye of the wind, where another roller drove us stern first along its crest. Pulling up in a groove of sea, we stowed trysail and set about making a drag, or hold-water, out of wood and weighted tarpaulin. Easing it over the port quarter, we tried lying-to stern first. The drag was a failure, and the bows were put back to the wind.

It grew cold, the barometer took a rapid dip, and rain fell on the sea. Dombey and I, holding to backstays, watched the craft and tried to solve our problem. The weather looked severe, and, with all thought of Bermuda gone for the moment, we saw with concern the heavy building up of the seas. Nearly always it is the seas that threaten the small sailer, just as usually it is the wind that finds the vital point in large sailing-ships. Some craft have not enough forefoot, or displacement forward, to heave to. The *Cimba* had, and we had to get her to ride with it safely. Time and again the foresheet was trimmed to a nicety, the helm adjusted, and then readjusted in the dark. After each change we waited, watching the result. Dawn found us still on deck, gripping to stays, studying the lively schooner as we drank from tins of condensed milk. An eternity of seas rose and fell between us and an east that glowed a windy sepia. It blew harder with the expanding light, and as it did we hit upon the best press that could be shown to the wind—a reefed foresail and a blanket set in the weather main rigging.

We stirred the fire in the stove and warmed the cabin. The work of the night had not been hard, not so hard as had been the waiting and watching between moves. In a small craft there is seldom enough physical work to stimulate the circulation. There is much of footwork, a lot of holding on, but even in tight moments agile fingers are as valuable as strong arms.

At half-past eight in the morning the wind moderated, the barometer held its own, then once more fell very slowly. The *Cimba* moved restlessly; the ocean brooded on some first thought. Overhead a pale sea of clouds ran to leeward, joining the storm-wrack twisted over the horizons. Straight-edged horizons had disappeared, to be replaced by a moving ocean's edge lifting and falling, sometimes seen, more often hidden by the streaming, uplifting water about us. Perhaps once every three minutes a sea, higher than its neighbours, would heave us to a dragging grey top, allowing a quick glance, a bird's-eye view, over wide distances, before again we were descending blank walls of cold, shadowless water.

The wind came back at Force 11 of the Beaufort Scale, moving everything before it. Only the schooner offered resistance as the seas, under a scud illuminated by weird yellow gale lights, bore down, rolling, gigantic, a full quarter of a mile from crest to crest. She stood before them, rakish, tar-daubed, her defense awaiting the attack.

WE DIDN'T TALK. A gale, as does a calm, induces silence. Often one of us would go up to watch the fight of the schooner, only to return to the cabin disappointed that there was nothing to do. They say that doing nothing is an art. If this is so, then the art must lie in overcoming the very hopelessness of the act. We cooked cracker hash, our last hot meal for some time, took turns at keeping vigil at the weather porthole, watched a whirling, telltale compass, and saw to it that spikes and sheath knives were handy. We broke silence to consider running off before the blow, deciding in the end that it was too dangerous, and under the conditions the last resort for a small craft.

BOATSWAIN. Heigh, my hearts! cheerly, cheerly, my hearts!
yare, yare! Take in the topsail! Tend to the master's whistle.
Blow, till thou burst thy wind, if room enough!

It was half-past two. I was glancing at Act One of the
very appropriate *Tempest* while drying out a last meagre ration of tobacco. Suddenly Dombey shouted from the port:
"Look at this sea!"

It must have been perpendicular! I felt the cabin lifting
as though striving for some great altitude. A second later
there was a thud, the deck slipped away beneath my feet,
careened, and the craft dived to a trough, falling down, as
though knocked beam-on along a great decline. The cabin
revolved, and we were driven against the bulkheads as amid
a deafening noise the hull went over, and we, together with
a thousand articles, were flung through space to crash on the
cabin-top, now upside-down. We fought our way out from
under a heavy heap, to find the cabin in darkness, the ports
under water. Looking up, I caught sight of the flooring over
my head; one of the floorboards dropped as I did so. Although the companion and the hatch, now leading into the
ocean, were closed, water came running in. Quite suddenly
the cabin filled with smoke as the ship's stove, bolted to the
floor and now overhead, emptied its coals and wood, to blaze
on the cabin roof; a stream of water poured out of the stove
from the submerged vent.

Why didn't she right herself? Not sure whether she had
not foundered, we knew intuitively that the ton of iron on

the keel, now up and down above us, was being offset by the weight of the masts, the bulk on the cabin carlings by the water that was filling her; and underneath the foresail was acting as a canvas fin, itself a keel of sorts.

We tried to stand up and handle the fires glowing in the semi-darkness, finding it difficult to keep a footing as we scooped water at the flames. The smoke increased, and we choked from the odours of kerosene, burning wood, and paper. There was the sound of another disturbance outside. We were hit again—thrown back to our knees. Once more the cabin swayed; we were tilted up against the bulkheads, pinned to them for a second, then dropped with a last stunning fall on to right-sided floorboards. The ocean is unbiased. A second wave had hit, causing the hull, which had gone over to port, to make a complete circle under water before coming up to starboard, to send the spars out of the sea and spinning back to windward.

We made the most of the chance. I groped about in the smoke, found a marline-spike, forced open the hatch, and reached the deck. All the gear stood; halyards and sheets trailed overside; but there was the foresail, still aloft, stiff and dripping wet. Waiting for a chance, I climbed aft and, while Dombey fought the fire, swung the *Cimba*, running her before it.

One look at the sea, and I knew that this was only the beginning, that the worst lay to windward, to the northwest. Presently I saw Dombey on deck furling the foresail. He came aft, shouted that the fire was out, and with hands on hips looked at the sea and gave a long whistle.

SIX

UNDER BARE POLES

THE *CIMBA* stormed along in a south-easterly direction, away from Bermuda, wet to her very trucks, her glistening masts and rigging offering windage enough to drive her rapidly to leeward. She needed no sail, and no sail could be set. Astern a tall lifting of grey would build up, close in; the bows would drop as the after-sections climbed, fighting to the steep level of the wave. For a moment it would appear that instead of rushing ahead she was making sternway up a vast slope of oncoming water. When it seemed that she could no longer hold the severe angle without pitch-poling—

drowning the bows and throwing counter and keel out of water—she would fight into the crest, to be attacked by grey-white water, broken, wild, to be sent skating, wedging over ocean for one hundred, two hundred, three hundred yards. Then the wave had gone, and she was falling again, falling under the steep shadow of the next sea.

For quarter of an hour Dombey and I, utterly silent, watched her every move. It was not as it had been before. We now sailed a ship that knew of defeat—a ship we had imagined undefeatable. We stood there fascinated by her spirited action, her effort, knowing, as we did, how much more courage is needed by the once defeated.

As she scudded we had to hold her directly behind the seas, which could be done only by facing aft into the blow, handling the tiller firmly, gingerly, never moving it much at any one time, although constantly shifting the rudder as though it were the tail of a fish. Steering on the slopes and in the troughs was not difficult, but when on a wave-top, with the hull surrounded by eddies shearing us first one way, then another, it was a different matter; then the helmsman dealt with two unseen forces, applying one, the invisible rudder, to offset the other, the invisible currents and roving counter-currents rushing the crest.

Atop the larger crests the hull would vibrate from keel to truck, as though a charge of dynamite had exploded close by, and at such times, with the rudder taking the brunt of the shock, it required not only two arms, but a strong back as well, to save the tiller from tearing free. In ordinary weather six-hour watches were held, and later we set what we called the '*Cimba* watch,' a twelve-hour wheel trick. But now, running before it as we were, watches were shortened to an hour. Partial exhaustion came on after the first fifteen minutes, and, cold though it was, a perspiration with it. The watch over, we would climb down to a wrecked cabin that no longer had bunks, jam ourselves against the skin, and even while holding a nautical prescience that the worst still lay to windward sleep soundly through the free hour.

COMING BELOW at midnight from another hour's wheel, I found the cabin still wet and damp, although nine hours had passed since the capsizing. Overhead charred areas stood out on the glistening paintwork. A swinging lamp with a cracked shade showed heaps of books, boxes, firewood, and bedding floating on the slop of the floorboards. I picked up *The Tempest*, soggy and dripping, then threw it back. The oven door banged open, and out flowed a small stream of water. Although my foot had gone through the frame, I saw the original *Cimba* still sailing on the bulkhead, and opposite Miss Landi looking down on the scene through tears of glistening sea-water.

After finding a tin of corned beef and opening it with an axe I began to consider our position. We were running before a long gale, now far from Bermuda, with no land between us and the African coast, with the water in one tank ruined, and that in the other tank almost gone. The blow was not moderating; not by any means. Yet we could not keep before it indefinitely, and on the first change for the better the craft must face it again.

She tore madly along a crest. The cabin vibrated with her thunder, and the lamp shadows dipped in swift, long arcs. She was labouring, trying hard to overcome defeat—the once beaten, striving out there in the dark to do so well in the cheerless gesture of just holding her own. Another un-muffled detonation about the hull; another. . . . I slept.

It seemed only a moment later when I was roused by the signal. One o'clock! I felt by the roll that it had grown worse. I had felt it in my sleep, as one is apt to do at sea.

For some unaccountable reason I opened the chronometer case bolted to the ship's skin. The chronometer, swinging in double gimbals, was ticking away as though nothing had happened, but, wonder of wonders, it was faced about so that the numeral 'six,' instead of 'twelve,' was at the top, a position that could be brought about only by the instrument simultaneously making two complete revolutions in the gimbals—a fore-and-aft one and an athwartships one. After taking a reading of the low barometer I went on deck.

"It's blowing up," said Dombey, through clenched teeth. Yes, there could be no doubt about it. On a convenient trough I took over the watch coat handed me, grasped the tiller, and, feeling Dombey's hand withdrawn from my back, knew that he had left for the cabin.

Into my face drove an eighty-mile wind, freezing and crying and sweeping down from the far-off ice-fields. The sky was naked, almost blue, and near its zenith a cold last-quarter moon shone light on to the crests of black waves, of waves travelling at high speed, now resembling tall cliffs, rather than mountains, cliffs formed by cutlass-like slashes of wind, ripped into storm patterns, now of a solid, ungiving black, now glowing in great fissures of infuriated silver, and sounding iron-like above the roaring wind.

My back was to most of the *Cimba*, to her bows, which were working every moment, to her bare masts resembling stunted arms raised against the night. I saw only that small area of after-deck, the paintwork beaded with frozen water picked out by the moon, the stiff parts of ropes, wet and shining on the narrow planking.

The waves built up in the moonlight, tightened, until the advancing slopes over which we had to rise became almost concave. Perhaps once a minute the schooner climbed a black slide of sea, once a minute fought a crest; then followed a brief breathing spell, of falling down a lee slope, of watching with fascination the growth of the next wave, majestic, mammoth, rolling rapidly out of a trough to swing mast-high, then more than mast-high. And in that pause I would wonder as to the climax of the gale, knowing that in its box of tricks there must be one supreme trick.

It is not true that a small craft can survive any weather, or that in storms she is always superior to a large ship. True, hers is the easier task in the average storm, for she rides atop waves the big ship labours through. Such waves, awe-inspiring as they are, have not the broken water at the apex to harm the smaller vessel; but there are others, waves an ocean cruiser may complete her life span without meeting, sufficient in broken water to confound any small craft, and in the end to overwhelm her illusive buoyancy—always her main defence. Fighters though they are, there is a foundering-point for all small craft.

At half-past one it became clear that the *Cimba* was near-ing hers as a storm from polar regions blasted over the ocean, warm with an opposing current. She raced on, spreadeagled from sea to sea, while I awaited the climax, still to windward. We had done what we could for her—a consoling thought in those moments. She had been moving too fast for safety; she still was, but now the lengths of a pair of cables trailed over the stern to restrain her somewhat. Storm oil had been needed, and, having none, we remembered that the old-fashioned engine had a central lubricating system, that con-sequently the tanks held a small amount of oil along with the petrol. Three jumpers, their arms and necks frapped, were stuffed with oakum and held under fuel-jets until sat-urated. Pricking them once or twice with a needle, we fas-tened lanyards about them, and secured one over the stern and one to either quarter, to ease the schooner appreciably.

At a quarter to two the long-awaited-for appeared. The *Cimba* climbed a wave, and, looking far to windward, I saw a black shape reared from horizon to horizon. As we dropped down a slope I knew that we were fated to meet the greatest sea I had ever come upon.

We climbed again, and I caught sight of its long moving body, already much nearer. This time as the schooner sank my heart sank with her. She was too small, too thin, for the purpose. I was minded to rouse Dombey, yet somehow did not do so. Instead I watched the inflexible purpose, the unfaltering purpose, of the wave, which now gleamed in one great moonlit plane, now darkened into heaving shadow, disappeared, lifted again, and rolled on and down towards us.

When it was still some distance off I could hear the roar of its cap above the gale. It closed in, travelling at eighty miles an hour, with a potential strength of thousands of pounds' pressure per square foot. As its half-mile body lifted black towards the moon, ranging to almost twice the height of the spars, I hurried my last preparations. Locking the tiller in a groove, I beat my hands on the coaming, warming them, and rubbed my eyes vigorously, that they would be at their best. Knowing that we were at least to be boarded, I lashed the mainsheet about my waist. Finally, after bracing my feet in the small well, knocking my fists a last time, and taking up the tiller, I was ready.

As the shadow of the wave reared above we began the journey up the almost perpendicular face. The *Cimba* went up rapidly, the ascent becoming steeper every instant. In the wild light the slope inverted to appear as a cavity, as a cave of sea-water. The sea was as black as pitch, and on it the white schooner fought for altitude, at such an angle that a man not holding to deck would have fallen clear forward and off the hull. The counter tilted upward in the moonlight, while far below the bows strove to withstand the pressure bearing upon them.

There was a great scream of wind, and, like a bad dream, over that black sea loomed a charge of white water. The *Cimba* struggled for the crest as the broken lip began to tremble, the body of the great sea to stagger. Just then arose a quarter wave—a portion of the main wave diverted to come bursting in at an angle to the wave proper. It was but little ahead of the main crest. Two things could be done— slew off course, taking the quarter sea properly over the stern, and chance getting back in position to meet the main wave, or hold course, ship the quarter sea, and trust to holding in line with the main flow.

I chose the latter. The quarter wave curled our way, a single cap of fluid silver hovering overhead, breaking to sweep the unprotected side. We were going over, so I jammed the tiller in a notch to have the craft more or less in line with the main sea should she work clear. The wave struck with immense impact, broke, rushed aboard, and, my lashing holding, I was driven head first and upside-down, to be jammed at the bottom of the well. As I tried to free myself, hampered by coat and sea-boots, I was not sure whether we had foundered or not, as for the second time that day I lost a sense of balance. I escaped from the water-filled well, saw the cold moon filmed with scud, the vessel, fighting beneath it, caught in the main crest—a leaping glitter, dangerous, rolling, roaring, and packing in against the struggling hull.

There was another scream of wind as the gale literally hurled the heavy white water at the schooner. I took the helm out of the notch and tried to guide her, standing waist-high in water, bracing arms with back; but the tiller was useless, absolutely useless, and I might as well have been holding to a walking-stick. Fearing for the rudder as the full force, of the sea struck, I slammed home the tiller in the midship notch. The wave picked us up and hurled us as though we were a match, so that I caught rapid visions of the moon, first on one quarter, then on the other.

The stern was sucked down; great areas of sea sought the vital decks. But the counter buoyed the surfaces, the bows fought as always they fought, and the stiff bilges underneath lifted and lifted. For three or four seconds I could not touch the tiller, during which her own buoyancy was all that could save the craft from being shattered, hove under.

The drive along the crumpling rim began. I freed the tiller, and as I put my weight against it felt the rudder-stock vibrating, the rudder quivering like a fin. Swinging through space from the altitude of the crest, I caught a glimpse of the surrounding ocean, far below, endless and empty, a distant heap of mounds, slow-rolling, cut by the great gleaming wind-slashes. The *Cimba* reeled in the flying wash, moving at utmost speed, while a wind as rare, as stinging, as that of a Himalayan gale blew against the thin wires of her rigging. With bow high, stern low, she planed, swinging with all her power in one long, exhilarating skid. Then suddenly the wave was beyond, and the *Cimba* was victoriously sinking to the trough. Glancing over my shoulder, I looked up to the receding form inclining in a tremendous slide of dragging foam to a crest, windy, shining. Already a quarter of a mile away, it made a freakish hinge towards the sky, tumbled, dropped in a smooth fall, and, with infinite majesty, glided into the oblivion to leeward.

ANOTHER SEA STRUCK at three o'clock. At four, while I was sleeping, a third wave rode us down. I awoke as the cabin reeled violently and the lamp blew out. Fearing for Dombey, I made for the hatch and looked out. But there he stood, bundled in the watch coat, the only silent form in all that confusion, composedly heaving on the tiller as though it were an oar and guiding the schooner safely down another slope.

At daylight it moderated, but only slightly, and for almost five hours more we were forced on under bare poles to an estimated position 165 miles west of Bermuda, blown completely off our only chart of the North Atlantic. At nine o'clock a consultation was held in the steering-well. Stores were low, water almost gone, and every hour that passed was taking us farther from the myth of land. The sea, still up-and-down, had fallen slightly. The time had come to attempt putting about and driving into the weather. One stood at the helm; the other double-reefed the mainsail. Timing it between two waves, we let the canvas press us around until, with jib and mainsail drawing, we headed to windward. The steep waves over which we had been sliding scenic-railway fashion now lunged at the bow, causing our motions to become sharp and rapid. With wet sails flattened in the wind the *Cimba* weaved and smashed a way into the white horses, travelling more like a submarine than a schooner. The wind appeared to be abating, causing the sea to loosen, until waves swelled in size, but waned in power. Then at nightfall the storm came back with much of its old strength, and after a quarter of an hour of futile fighting we went on the defensive and hove to.

"Again!" shouted Dombey.

"And again!" I echoed, furling the jib. And out of the night came a third echo, an ironic undertone of wind.

After much effort the stove was lighted, and a hot meal cooked, of ship-bread and corned beef mixed into a hash. Drinking-water was doled out with care. We had neither coffee nor tea, both ruined in the capsizing. There was no tobacco. The meal over, we began a watch-and-watch, and, slightly nauseated by an odour of kerosene, were only too glad to stay out in the weather, still cold and now accompanied by rain.

On the morning of the next day we again set canvas against the blow. The fisherman put her heart into the scheme, shattering a staggering, lumpy sea, wetting her sails in a blunt attempt at headway. Her gear strained as she swung up and into the drive of water, her masts over to leeward, while the gentle curved bows hammered into broken, streaming waves. For an hour she plunged west with trembling luffs, biting into sea after sea in a wet uphill hack. Then, in a rising Force 9 gale, for the eighth time since departure we hove her to, bringing the total number of hours in this position to over a hundred and thirty.

Through all of a day, in which ponderous ghosts of seas loomed from out of the rain-light to moan, burst, and disappear, endlessly, and through a night of flying rain the schooner lay with her head under her wing. We, her two attendants, took care of her few wants, standing vigil round the clock.

And then the morning and the totally unexpected— morning and a sun climbing a clear sky to warm a gleaming sea of blue. Sail was swung aloft to the gentle wind, and we ran a shining sea of the long-lost, straight-edged horizons. The sun warmed the decks, dried the sails, and the *Cimba*, her red paint cutting blue water, slid to the west.

Before noon course was altered to north—we considered ourselves once more on the chart—and again preparations were made for a landfall. At twelve the phantom of a ship, an oil-tanker, the first vessel sighted since the liner, was seen far off on the horizon. There was a temptation to follow her. At least she was headed somewhere, while we—well, we were only searching. But Dombey had a hunch, the result of a handful of sights and good dead reckoning, and, I agreeing, we held our way, dropping the tanker out of sight.

Ever since taking departure the two of us had worked hand-to-hand in perfect co-ordination under the tension. The arrival of good weather did not lessen this tension, which until Bermuda was raised would even increase. So, sharing but one thought in common, we worked together on the weathered deck, flattening the salted sailcloth, setting up the rigging.

At four o'clock I climbed the mainmast and looked for land. Nothing was seen; not even a gull hovering over the calm ocean. It grew on to sunset; the colours brightened in the west, paled on the sea; shadows grew longer, the light wind lighter. It was time for another consultation.

The way in which land is picked up from the deck or rigging of a small craft is always fascinating. The land does not slowly appear out of mist, nor does it come suddenly to stand boldly on the horizon. Rather, it first appears as a vision, as a happy portent arriving out of thin air, out of a vastness of space, to lie with utter humility upon the curved lip of the sea. First it is not there; then, at the flick of an eyelash, there it is, a flimsy mirage that may or may not be more than a low and wandering cloud.

Beneath the leaning mast the shadows became darker on the pear-shaped deck. There was Dombey in the cockpit, from time to time giving me an impatient glance. The schooner seemed to be moving easily, her way slowed by the falling wind. Beyond her some porpoises played on the pale water. Presently they were gone, and the ocean was empty. The wind drew off, and the schooner stopped in a silence broken by the clatter of her gear; then a slight breeze, the masts leaning, the hull beginning to murmur through water. In the west a cloud burst into sudden flame to flare over the immutable plane, now dark, outsweeping to the sky. And under the cloud, touching the sea, something appeared—another cloud, the slight blur, the low, unmoving vision! I came down the shrouds, and Dombey, jumping from the tiller, caught my hand. We were happy, demonstrative. And then, quite unexpectedly, there happened a very strange thing—Dombey and I in a dispute, in a dispute over some absurdly trivial matter. Bermuda had been raised, the tension snapped!

Before starlight the scents of distant earth were floating in the wind. Our difference had passed like an aimless squall, and together we watched the vision change shape and size, and, later, the shining lights flaring on the low body.

The wind was little more than a breath by the time St David's Head was abeam. We sailed up to a lighted ship, H.M.S. *Scarsborough*, anchored some way off-shore. There was only one figure on deck, a middy. We hailed him. Had he any tobacco? The sight of a lonely northern schooner appearing out of the night manned by a crew making such a request surprised him, to say the least. Without a word he ran below, returned, and, still silent, threw something into the mainsail. Tobacco and papers! We thanked him and headed on, leaving him still speechless upon the deck.

The chart of the approach to St George's Channel had been ruined in the capsize by tar, coal-dust, syrup, and cocoa, and to pilot the *Cimba* I had to fall back on a knowledge of the waters learned in boyhood.

Gliding into harbour, we found the town asleep in the dark armlike hills of cedar, and only one or two lights left burning above the water. A few drops of rain fell, but save for their beat and the creak of the gaffs aloft there was utter silence. The *Cimba* ghosted by Ordnance Island, and, bringing up at Market Wharf, closed her voyage.

The Square, except for a sleepy coloured boy, was deserted, the soft forms of its buildings appearing unreal, like the darkened scene of an ended play. The boy saw us, woke up, and ran into the White Horse Tavern, just closing for the night. A stalwart figure came out by the lighted doorway, hurrying towards us.

"Is it the *Cimba*?" "Is it the *Cimba* turned up?"

Yes, she had turned up after half a month of sea adventure in weather that had sunk a forty-five-foot schooner, a sixty-five-foot ketch, and a four-masted schooner, all close by her. She had turned up after the officers of Bermuda-bound liners had held no hope for her in the December gales; to win after first losing, and in the end to make port under her own canvas, without a leak, without a strained spar, without a torn sail.

SEVEN

ON TO GRAND TURK

O lovely form of undismayed desire;
　O vagabond, whom no dull thrift delays;
　Flying as wishes fly, on magic ways;
Knowing no limit save the sunset's fire!
　　　From "To the Yacht 'Whim,'" by M. P. HUDDLESTON

MORNING, and the harbour green and waving over purple shoal, the sky stretching, a calm, illuminated sea, above white roofs and trees cool with shadow. After a sleep ashore and hot baths we felt as fresh as the day itself, and walked as though on air down a limestone road to the schooner.

Climbing aboard, we set sail, and, working over a glowing slide of water, secured her amid a fleet of ancient wrecks. Then Dombey and I moved ashore to "Caledonia," the home of my uncle and aunt, leaving the schooner to wait patiently, guarded from wind by useless, worn-out hulls. Experience, hoary age, and infinite wisdom lifted high above her—crumbling masts, Samson's-posts, and great broadsides of metal, teak, and wormed pine—while old rigging whispered of a lost, a romantic youth. On a night of southerly winds the fleet could be heard complaining—a groan from a half-filled hold, the creak of an unbraced yard working on a rusted parrel, and less distinct sounds, the 'talk' of damaged ships. Morning would find them silent, motionless in sunshine, like a squadron thrown up by a departed hurricane—the French barquentine *Fraternité*, white-boned and broken; a down-east schooner that had turned turtle and drowned her crew; the teak hull of H.M.S. *Ready*, sloop-of-war, her Majesty's brasswork turned green, almost black; the decommissioned *Gladisfen* (now gone)—the "Rooster," as she was devotedly called. Beyond on the glittering harbour lay the most favoured of the fleet—one still moving to wind—the beautifully modelled *Duncrag*, once a barque, now a hulk, coal-laden.

St George's, small centre of Bermuda's East End, sliding like a limestone wave into a harbour held to the north by its white arm, to the south by the malachite reach of St David's, is steeped in the traditions of the sea. Long ago, while serving as a rendezvous for freebooters of the West India trade, and later for Confederate blockade runners, a hundred sail swung to anchors in its harbour. Steam replaced sail, and the port became a coaling station. Oil replaced coal, vessels covered more ocean without bunkering, and suddenly St George's lost her ships. But not the traditions. No, they linger on in a town fortunate in having as mayor the Hon. William Meyer, a true lover of the sea.

Not all of the old craft are idle. Several cedar fishing sloops and freight boats are active, some after a century of work. They have outlived the Bermudian racing dinghies, those fabulous fourteen-footers stepping twenty-eight feet of mast, with bowsprits the length of the hull and booms even longer. Demanding immaculate boatsmanship, the dinghies were the offspring of native designers, creators of the Marconi sail, the Genoa jib, who built craft unrivalled in speed until the Victorian era was well under way. A dinghy race between the two harbours, St George's and Hamilton, once drew large gatherings of spectators from every part of the island. But those days are gone, the remaining dinghies lie unused, and yachting flourishes only in Hamilton, in boats of foreign design, fine, delicate craft, more becoming the grandeur of continents than the simplicity of islands.

One bright February morning Dombey and I sailed out of the harbour and pointed for Tucker's Bay and the Flats. On arriving the craft was cradled on a marine slip—the second she had known, the last she was to encounter. The top-sides were painted, the after-deck covered buff, the forward white. After a thorough washing both cabins were given a coat of grey from the floor to the level of the bunk-tops; the rest was trimmed white, and then, feeling the urge, we striped the carlings blue. The schooner's under-body was given a coat of bitumastic—an experiment against teredo worms—and two coats of red copper, not quite meeting the raised water-line, now red, striped black. Then the *Cimba* was launched and sailed back to St George's, where the gaff was removed from the mainmast and the sail recut as a jib-headed mainsail, a change never regretted. Masts were scraped, slushed down with tallow, and the craft, spick and span, looking a trifle overpainted, was once again ready for sea.

Fifty pounds of ship's biscuit and a hundred tins of corned beef; onions, carrots, potatoes, marmalade, arrowroot, tinned milk, tea, flour; Marmite and Bovril (concentrated foods for emergencies), lime-juice and cocoa; bags of fragrant cedar firewood, bedding-grass, fuel, and tank-water—all to help us on our way to the West Indies. Most of the provisions were sealed in twenty big biscuit-tins stowed in the after-cabin as so much cargo. An amount of miscellaneous gear came from strange sources: a gimballed cabin lamp from the wrecked *Taifon*, a second, of the vintage of 1873, from the stout German barque *Dorothea*; a tarpaulin, which would serve as an awning, and a halyard, to be used as an anchor cable, from the full-rigged ship *Benjamin F. Packard*. Already we had also a collection of good-luck pieces. Besides Frank Jaeger's silvered horseshoe, nailed over the low chart table, we were presented with an ivory lion, an elephant, a camel, two four-leafed clovers, a lucky dime, nickel, and threepenny-bit, a penny, two house flags, the racing silks of the island's most famous dinghy, the *Victory*, a little silver cross, and a bottle of brandy.

March 17, 1934. We were ready to leave for Grand Turk, the Island of Salt, bearing south 28 degrees west, some six hundred miles over ocean. Dombey and I stood on Market Wharf a last time while the schooner, breasted alongside, flew the identification signals of the first *Cimba*, the code flags R, K, V, and S. A well-wisher, one of the small group on the wharfside, went on board and knotted a streamer of green ribbon to the eye of the jib-stay.

"Stand by! Stand by!" The launch *Troubadour* had come alongside to tow us to sea. The group on the wharf boarded her. The launch moved ahead, urging us over the harbour, and as it did so I recalled my first boat, the *Owl*, a comrade of a boyhood when every island held treasure, and the borders of this blue harbour were the borders to all of the world. The tug *Powerful* and the steamer tender blew farewell, and we had passed into Castle Harbour for the ocean ahead. Again I recalled how when only seven a hurricane overwhelmed a cat-boat in which I sailed, the first blast snapping the mast, scuttling the boat. I remembered my uncle aiding me in the pull for the shore, the shrieking of the wind, and, finally, the dark shelter of an abandoned house, heavy with the odour of onions.

And then suddenly land was astern, the launch was heaving in open sea, and it was time to part company. We cast off the towline, set sail, blew a blast with the fog-horn, and as the motor-boat ran for the Castle Roads headed to sea.

From the very first the recut mainsail acted well. It showed less area aloft than the old spread, while a cloth had been removed from the leech to bring the sail entirely inboard, a feature unusual in a schooner. The smaller spread did not affect the speed, a fact heartening us as we prepared to run heavy through the north-east trades. How many miles could be covered in twenty-four hours? An able cruiser, even a small one, should make 140 miles under favouring conditions, although each single mile beyond that is difficult to gain. To reach the 150's and 160's requires almost perfect wind, while the 170's lie beyond the average cruiser. Nevertheless two voyagers, a Norwegian sloop and an American, had far exceeded this by tieing for a record run of 196 miles. Both of these craft were larger than we; moreover, our areas were small, capped by no square sail, the most powerful plane for running down-wind.

The puffs swung to the south; the day wore on. At five a skyline of almost pure jade became smudged with black squalls. They threatened, then drew off. The sun sank, and soon the *Cimba* was plunging her side-lights through the darkness. Supper: hot tongue, potatoes, biscuit, China tea.

That night the craft steered herself, the helm being handled only to tack in midnight airs. The wind drew off, indicating that we should have done better had we waited before sailing until it veered south-west, as in March it often holds that direction for a day or two before a rapid clockwise shift to the south.

Throughout the next day and the day following we were harnessed by light head-winds, held in their irons while ghosting upon loose sea-wash. The *Cimba*, sailing herself, passed over 207 miles of ocean, striving for the border of the trade winds, her crew slowly regaining a co-ordination with her motions, limbering backs and shoulder muscles; for no matter how long one has sailed the first few sea days find one imperfectly adjusted to the rhythms, the confining spaces, of a ship.

The third day began with moderate breezes shifting south. The glass fell, and we looked for the trouble which started at lunch-time—rain-squalls, a rising wind, and a sea rolling a sharp chop. At two, with the wind increasing fresh to strong, the straining foresail was handled. It came on heavier, and half an hour later we hove-to under a new combination, a double-reefed mainsail, a storm trysail on the fore, as grey seas, slow of body, their crests flying, coasted by in the pelting rain. "*Cimba* luck!" we sighed, going below.

From the log. "5.00 P.M. Wind reaching gale force. Ship riding comfortably. . . ." The cabin looked cheery in the swinging light thrown by the lamps of the *Dorothea* and *Taifon*, and smelled pleasantly of the burning cedar in the stove. It was a homely dugout, resembling a little kitchen rather than the cabin of a deep-water cruiser. We talked about our capsize, wondering if it could have been avoided. It could not have been, we decided, changing the subject to the bright Bermudian days, now astern.

The line storm lasted almost twenty-four hours before a shift to the north-west, when we set sail in a Force 7 wind to run down seas still powerful and capped. That night the jib steadying the bows was trimmed, the reefs shaken.

I came on deck early the next morning to find the seas a great confusion of blue, exploding, white-capped, the sun lighting the sweep out to the horizons, and the wind, blowing under an immense light of turquoise, driving us south over broken sea. The north-east trades were here! They were too far aft to wing us at our best, but even so, as I took the tiller from Dombey, the *Cimba* smoked, holding a flashing bone in her teeth. Now on the horizon to windward clouds, small and distant like the studding-sails of a *Flying Dutchman*, hove in sight, sailed down, scudded overhead, huge, sun-drenched, rushing to leeward faster than the white-wooded schooner over the rich, windy ocean. The masts glistened, the backstays tautened, and sails and clouds moved across a bright sky. The *Cimba* was fetching flying-fish weather, to run with a long, loping rhythm for the West Indies.

Smoke was sighted on the horizon early in the afternoon,

and soon we raised a small steamer. Even though her course would hold her some five miles off, I called Dombey to see her. Through the glasses we made out a Bull Line freighter, bound east from the Gulf. To our surprise a moment later she altered course in our direction. She closed in and ranged abeam; we dipped the ensign and drew away, a strong wind ripping at our cloths. Looking astern, we were once more surprised. The steamer had stopped. Rounding into the wind, we drove for her lee.

"Can we assist you?" a voice was roaring from the bridge. Assist us! The captain and his mate awaited our answer. The steamer rolled, her waist lined with seamen and firemen.

"May we have a position?"

"Here it is," and one of the figures on the bridge shouted the steamer's latitude and longitude. "Anything else?"

"Will you report the *Cimba*, seven days out from St George's, Bermuda, bound for Turks Island, all well?"

"And anything else?"

We had not time to answer as the *Cimba*, making rapid sternway in the eye of the wind, carried us beyond earshot. There was a short, good-humoured blast from the steamer's whistle. One or two seamen waved diffidently; one handled a camera. Then we saw the propeller of the S.S. *Elizabeth* turning over, lashing the blue water beneath her black stern. She went back to her business, and we, after resuming course, watched her pass towards the horizon on her thankless task of carrying cargo from landsmen to landsmen.

How different had been the meeting with that South America-bound liner! "Oh, the liner, she's a lady, without the manners of a tramp. . . ."

Our run for the day had been a good one, 140 miles from noon to noon, but by no means the best the schooner could do. We had not made the 150's, and were certainly a long way from the higher runs. However, the wind was quartering, increasing, and in a last attempt before landfall we hurried to the southward under mainsail and steadying jib.

All through the day the *Cimba* raced before a West Indian chocolate gale, baring her red-and-black boot-topping, climbing and planing with intense effort, her sails curved and gripping the wind as the cotton raked stiff-bunted under the glowing sky. Sunset, and she continued to sweep down miles, lurching into the night of an old moon, which made the swing of the sea appear as a rush of green and bronze, with scattered crests, rolling brass-headed, flaming in hazy light. Her bows gashed the living sea; her entire underbody thundered. And in the morning she was still storming onward, straining, overeager, a flash of wake screwing astern in the early sunshine, her mainsail skin-tight and biting at the backstays. Noon found Dombey, sextant in hand, taking last sights before landfall. She was still moving, and I held her with a stiff helm. The computations followed, and then reckoning was checked for error. In the last windy twenty-four hours the *Cimba*, under main and jib, had made 198 miles!

A hundred and ninety-eight miles in a day! A hundred and one miles in twelve hours! Oh, it was good all right! Good to see these items in the logbook of a simple, unvarnished ship; in the log of a half-pint schooner hailing from a humble, never known port—something left over from another century, from time past, born of a true humility, which is, and always will be, the essence of all true nobility. It was good to see them—these items that meant so little to the world, so much to the crew.

At the end of another sunset, when only a handful of miles from our destination, we joined forces at the steering-well, sipped tea from tin cups, and shared the landfall watch. The craft drove on under a vast, a punctuated fire of windy stars, while the trades, bearing down, whined in the tophamper, hinting at some magical liberty, some living freedom beyond the eternal horizons. And with the tea still hot in our mugs we picked up an isolated eye of light, just above sea-level, dimmed and dwarfed by the stars.

We lay off and on the Grand Turk beacon until daybreak, then headed for the low island. When on soundings a Negro pilot came on board, dressed in the attire of a battleship's commander. We sailed towards the open roadstead. The sands of the shore drew nearer, the blue water paled to lime, the sails fell muffled down the spars, and a black anchor, making an arc over the bows, splashed into the peaceful water.

EIGHT

THE CARIBBEAN AND
BREAK-UP PORT

GRAND TURK is flat, unpretentious. Stunted shrub covers most of a plain which I recall being dominated by seven palms lifting from a small hill, the Look-out. Three of the narrow coasts bordering the plain are beached, but the east shore, with its dangerous offing, is rocky and swept by large seas. The lee side of the island holds the settlement, where a Government jetty protrudes from an area of open ground called Salt Square. Here a road starts, which on passing the wooden frames of one or two general stores, a post-office, and a cable office wanders into bush and cactus. Behind this road runs a second, groping through a cluster of cabins occupied by Negroes working the salt ponds. There are three ponds, arranged with a system of sluices and traps to drain off the pickle, which in time becomes the rock-salt used by Banks fishermen for their catch.

The *Cimba* lay quietly at anchor off the jetty. She never came to appear as an offensive intruder amid any group of native shipping, regardless of how humble a fleet might be. Not that she gave an appearance of meekness, for, typical of her kind, she had her own peculiar air of rakishness and daring; but a simplicity of rig and equipment, accentuated by her slight size, endowed her with the virtues of the unobtrusive—yes, even among the vagabond trading sloops wandering to the Grand Turk roadstead with oranges from the west, pink coral pearl, mangoes, and sponge. Most of them were unpainted, misshapen, with warped spars clumsily stayed by a tangle of old sisal-rope, telephone wire, even barbed fencing-wire. One sloop, judged to be near the end of her sailing days, turned out to be not six months old. It was a mystery how they ran through their squalls, and on thinking of it one was likely to recall Winslow Homer's picture *The Gulf Stream*—a stump of mast, sharks circling a rolling hull, and a big black native stretched in the stern sheets, along with some lengths of warped sugar-cane.

The only navigating paraphernalia used by the native skippers is an antiquated compass. They have no charts, no sextants, and although sailing lengthy gaps of open water they would part with the compasses were it not for prohibiting regulations. I showed one skipper the first chart of the West Indies he had seen. "Damned if I knew she looked like that there, sir!" And, looking up from it half an hour later, he reflected, "She's pretty near to right, sir. Pretty near."

Dombey and I made Miscick, a young native, the conscientious watchman of the schooner, and went ashore for a few days to the home of Mr and Mrs Peter Smith, of the Cable Station. There was only one trouble with Miscick: he was far too painstaking, following us about, step by step, with a damp soogee rag, his one regret being that the *Cimba* had no brasswork: it could have been made to shine gaudily in that pleasant sun.

The days ashore were spent in swimming, wandering on the beaches, occasionally trying a hand at tennis, sometimes in doubles, sometimes in vicious battles between ourselves. We called on Governor Hutchings and his daughter, and boarded the old *Mayflower*, the ex-racing fisherman of Boston, now serving as the island's mail vessel. With an added third mast and fifteen feet removed from an ample counter the *Mayflower* still has a turn of speed, and on one occasion made the run to Kingston in four days.

Turks Island is a happy place, and although we would have stayed longer our thoughts wandered to Panama, the port where many an ocean cruise is abandoned. Break-up Port! Until we had reached there, weathered it, and gained the Pacific, we could not feel the voyage more than begun. So on the 2nd of April the *Cimba* hauled west and stood away for the Windward Passage and Jamaica. She over-hauled a sloop, put her hull-down, safely passed the Endymion Banks, fetched the Haitian coast and Cape St Nicholas Mole, to enter the Windward Passage, where the run continued in lighter airs.

On my sunrise watch the third morning out I sighted a sail over the starboard bow. The *Cimba*, working in light winds, closed in until an hour later, when I made out a large two-masted schooner, fidding topmasts, evidently bound for Kingston on a heading corresponding to our own. Suddenly she fell off-wind to yaw first one way, then another. I thought her out of control, but the glasses revealed a man at the wheel. Dombey came up to find us altering course and standing directly after the stranger; but no sooner was our heading changed than figures appeared on the vessel's decks to trim sail and head, not for Jamaica, but north-west, towards the Cuban coast. She passed out of sight, leaving us at a loss regarding the manoeuvre.

The *Cimba* sailed up the winding length of Kingston's harbour to come alongside Myer's Rum Wharf, three and a half days out from Turks, several hours ahead of the old *Mayflower's* time. Kingston proved the most demanding, the most expensive port at which we were to call. All the first day I was kept busy between the Customs House and the Port Captain's office. But the worst came when a black policeman was stationed to keep an officious eye on us throughout our stay, an arrogant individual whom before leaving I fear we gave cause to regret his officiousness.

After a trip into the high Jamaican hills we left for Panama, racing down-harbour against a large yacht, a sloop of the Royal Jamaican Yacht Club, which with a crew of ten was out to illustrate good-naturedly the difference between racing and cruising. But she failed, for in the end the *Cimba* ran down-wind to overhaul the larger craft, beating to windward and leaving her rival beyond hailing distance.

She ghosted steadily into the south, carrying the mood of the dying trades, sliding through vacuums of intense blue, her spirit laid bare by the sun and shrouded by misty nights of sleeping seas. At the end of the fifth day she glided into Limon Bay, the Atlantic entrance to the Panama Canal, five days out from Kingston, seventeen days a few hours from Bermuda.

Twenty-four hours later her crew, shaved and dressed in whites, rowed the collapsible tender to the shore. The night was warm, the air still and heavy. Passing the aisles of administration buildings, silent under rows of royal palms, we crossed the American boundary, entering the native town of Colon, a haze of scarlet-and-orange light streaming fan-shaped from the doorways of cabarets, bars, fruit shops. Here were noise, happy confusion, wealth and dazed poverty, sought-after comforts and unsought-for dangers; here was civilization again, out for the evening, dressed in its best and blinded by its own lights. A crowd was passing and repassing the doorways, elegant, hopeful, assured, like the blind made happy, like the old made young, searching, searching once more. A neon sign flashed "Atlantic Cabaret" over a street-corner. From the silence of a side-street came an exploding burst of laughter, passing off into echoes. American sailors, fruit-sellers, dark, birdlike Spaniards in white pongee, dance-hall girls, the firemen off some German merchantman, lottery-sellers, and young Panamanians, arrogant and smoking marihuana. Silks and satins, gay and flowered, dungaree, linen, and khaki swung past the streaming lights. The sound of jazz came from a balcony overhead. The sharp, animated noise of castanets. The slapping of coins on wood. A loud cough from behind a closed shutter. The clatter of billiard-balls; sharp cries and echoes of Latin laughter. And the sound rose towards the dark sky—a murmur—one moment a caress, the next vindictive and threatening. "Let's have some fun!"

In the morning we took a berth at one end of Limon Bay, facing the unfinished French canal, a muddy reach running through a yellow jungle and lined by rusted dredges. On the surrounding water lay a group of dingy craft—abandoned ocean cruisers, destined to voyage no more. They had been hard sailed to the Canal with the best intentions of swinging out over the Pacific for a drive to the South Seas. And then something had occurred, causing their crews to abandon the plan. Was it the Canal itself—a psychological hurdle of ponderous concrete, joining two oceans, yet capable of dividing the urge propelling these ventures by bringing about indecision? With the locks once passed there could be no turning back. But, no, likely the trips fell to more material shortcomings—a lack of proper equipment for cross-ocean journeys, weakened finances, unfit craft. The vessels lay on the brown water of Break-up Port, with canvas mildewing, with decks silent and deserted. "One . . . two . . . three . . ." counted big Dombey, making out two sloops, a schooner, a pair of yawls, four ketches.

While beaching an open boat in muddy water I was bitten either by a conger-eel or a barracuda, the natives not deciding which. From the hospital I was taken to the home of our good friends Mr and Mrs Tucker McClure, whose native servant, by putting strips of raw sword cactus on the wound, had me up and about in two weeks' time.

For a while we disappeared from Limon Bay, standing towards the San Blas Archipelago, ghosting into such ports as Nombre de Dios, Isle Grande, Porto Bello. We worked amid the hot calms of the Spanish Main, came to know its windless nights, its nights of mysterious squalls; pushed the schooner against head-currents, manoeuvred her into shoal-water, beached her for painting, and lost every plate aboard and the only pair of binoculars in what came to be known as the "ninety-dollar squall." We deviated up rivers, along silent banks of damp jungle, and by the time the *Cimba* picked up old moorings had learned rudiments in trading for pine-apples, pigs, and yams.

Shortly after sunrise on the 17th of June we started engine to run the Canal, making for Gatun Locks, the first of the three to be passed. The services of a pilot had been declined on paying the moderate Canal fee of ten dollars, five of which went to an admeasurer, five for each ton displaced. We asked Mr Tucker McClure, with us for the day, to steer in the wake of a large 200-ton topsail schooner, the yacht *La Korrigane*, of Bordeaux, also bound for the South Pacific. A big Grace steamer slid by, the *Santa Rosa*, one of those modern ships that to look complete need only a winding-key protruding from the stack. A massive wall of coloured steel, she led the way into the yawning lock, where electric mules were soon nursing her up the concrete breach. The *La Korrigane* followed, held to the centre by warps, two forward, two aft; then came the *Cimba*, snubbed to the right-hand side of the lock by a pair of lines handled by a native labourer, high above our mastheads.

Every one hurried to prepare for the rising water. The mules groaned under the liner's flanks; the Frenchman's afterguard gave sharp orders to the shore crew. We worked to secure six rubber-tyre fenders to starboard. Holding the worst position of all, the schooner was kept to the after-end of the lock almost directly over vents soon to be alive with water filling the chamber, a thousand feet long, a hundred wide, at the rate of a foot a minute.

Lines were bowsed in; the confusion of voices increased. Our line handler gave one lazy glance down from the concrete rim and suddenly disappeared. A shadow fell over the *Cimba*, and I turned to see a steel gate, appearing as a part of the sky itself, moving above us, closing on our flanks. Oh, yes, of course! It was shutting out the Atlantic. There in the distance was the dingy fleet of Break-up Port, deserted on a mud flat sparkling with sunshine. And beyond the now invisible Atlantic of victories and defeats, of gains and losses, disillusion and everlasting fascination. The gate came together; the shouting died down. In another second we should be in trouble, for the two lines leading up and down could not possibly hold us snubbed against the wall, while a third, to span the chamber, had been denied us. Just then the lock became very nearly silent.

The water came in one violent uprush. The *La Korrigane*'s lines parted, and I saw her slew at high speed, driving stern first into the concrete, smashing her timber. The *Cimba* sheared to the centre of the lock, acting as if she were being hurriedly run over a bumpy road, turned erratically, and in an overwhelming eddy dived at amazing speed for the side of the lock. She lunged into the masonry, and her bow, unprotected by a fender, hit fairly, with an impact that threw us from our feet. She backed off into the gyrating water. She turned once more, and lunged for the wall. Dombey sweated on a straining warp, while I cut loose a fender in time to jam it between concrete and hull. And then, the chamber filling, our shore-lines became effective.

The lock gained, we headed for the next, Miraflores, stopping the engine and setting sail. Steamer upon steamer passed, looking out of place amid the green jungle. The *Santa Rosa* rushed out of sight, disappearing from above the vegetation, an impetuous monster which, for all its speed, was late—for ever late! The French yacht, far ahead, came to a stop. As we closed in we wondered how much she had been damaged. A figure on the poop raised a speaking trumpet.

"Stand by. We'll give you a tow."

"We're all right. The engine's working. We only cut it to sail."

"Let's tow you anyway"—cheerily.

"Thank you. Are you badly hurt?"

"Only a small dry-dock job. Nothing at all, really." She must be heavily built; not many large yachts could have taken the punishment without losing an entire counter.

Evening: stars burning over the still masts, a wind scented with ship smells, the odours of tropical wood, wandering haphazardly into space. The long day was done. Mr Tucker McClure had gone, and the *Cimba* floated for the first time in the Pacific. It had been a full day—a collision, a sail in the Canal, a tow, a new port, and, lastly, a new ocean.

At Balboa enough equipment and stores were taken on to last to Tahiti, five thousand miles away. We rove off new running rigging, and added to a small reserve of sails two short-footed spinnakers—wingsails, as they came to be known. The water-supply was increased by lashing to the waterways the fifteen-gallon tank from the ill-fated *Thelma*, a sloop wrecked on Cocos Island, as well as by making fast to the gallows frame an additional small pine keg. While most of the stores were bought at the Cristobal Commissary, managed by the obliging Mr Brown, some were shipped at Balboa—flour, corn-meal, tinned beef, milk, onions, ship's biscuit, tinned potatoes, for cold-storage ones quickly rot. Bacon, eggs, butter, and coffee were luxuries too dear for the trip. Marmalade replaced butter; tea and cocoa took the place of coffee. Such excellent sea-fare as salt pork and cod were abandoned because of the amount of fresh water required to prepare them. A thousand rounds of 30.30 ammunition for the Winchester, a hundred odd charts, from Panama to Singapore, a Primus or Swedish stove to replace the coal stove; tallow, white lead, fish-oil, spare canvas, and marline completed the list.

The *Cimba* was beached, and we gave her two coats of copper, in our haste finishing the work by lantern-light. The *La Korrigane* sailed, her crew expressing the hope of meeting us in the Galapagos. I came down with some kind of a fever, and as my leg had still to heal fully a postponement of plans seemed certain. Then more friends of the *Cimba's*, Mr and Mrs Alfred Marvin, took me in charge, and finally all was ready. Last negotiations were made with the officials, and the white *Cimba*, with but eleven inches of freeboard amidships, heading into a July sunset, moved slowly out on to the greatest sea of all.

NINE

HACKING TO WINDWARD

There's a schooner in the offing,
With her topsails shot with fire,
And my heart has gone aboard her
For the Islands of Desire.

RICHARD HOVEY, *The Sea Gypsy*

FOR TWO days we hung off the Perlas Islands, thirty miles
from Panama, on an unrewarded quest for fish. On the 7th of
July we set sail for the Galapagos, some eight hundred miles
to the south-west. The day passed slowly, a day echoing with

the clacking of sheet-blocks and the jingle of loose travellers wrenching at plough-steel deck-horses. At times the becalmed craft stood absolutely motionless, as though propped underneath by invisible shoring; then suddenly, disturbing the reverie of a dingy sea curiously littered with driftwood, she would shake her hanging sails and begin to march.

We were not going to try breaking through the great inertia these waters know in the rainy season by making a straight-lined track to the Galapagos. Instead a right-angled course was planned, keeping within a hundred miles of the South American coast, using whatever land wind spiralled off the Andes, holding almost due south until fetching the horse latitudes. Then the course would be west, seaward, and towards the Galapagos, to end a fourteen-hundred-mile drive that should bring a smarter passage than the direct route.

Squalls heavy with rain closed the second and third days. Typical of their kind, the low-latitude squalls arrived in groups, so that often we would be in company with a dozen or more at one time. Some were smudged, cloudlike, others, fully defined, slanting vertically over the sea, shifting in cyclonic movement, those to windward rarely attacking, while many lunged up under the lee to send us flying on our way. There would be a great wailing of wind, a heavy rain, the scuppers would break water, the sheets would cut their rigid blocks, and suddenly the gust would be gone, leaving the helmsman to screw the rain from his eyes, and cast off his so-called oilskins—in reality Nova Scotian rubber suits, drier, less awkward, safer, than oilskins.

On the fourth day out Panama lay 210 miles astern. Squalls made us take wind from every compass-point, pay off sheets to erratic puffs, and jam into wet thrusts of re-volving winds. The grey unlighted Colombian coast would appear in the offing, then mysteriously draw off, leaving an empty space of water reaching out to the groove of sky.

The *Cimba* could ghost, even though the masts were little more than stumps holding upright her pocket-handkerchief sails. Deep-laden, not too far from being awash at the rails, she would catch a puff, then lose it, the heavy load carrying her hundreds of yards over windless space. Always on the verge of being becalmed, she but rarely stopped sailing, and at times seemed to carry a way only through utter persis-tence, a dogged will that would force a smile from the criti-cal helmsman. I couldn't say how favourably her ghosting qualities compared with those of other cruisers—not too well, perhaps—but I do know that for sheer tenacity she could hold her own with any afloat.

From the log. "July 11, A.M.: Heavy squalls upon us from the south. Sail handled quickly. P.M.: Wind high and chopped seas, gradually diminishing to light variables." Twenty-five miles were made good. The next day was calm, sultry, but the morning following saw the return of head-winds and brought sharp lightning from the distant coast. The wind held south, and we began working tacks to seaward at night, changing to inshore ones throughout the day, sailing into a head-current, a portion of the cold Humboldt sweep flowing up from the far-away Horn.

When a good grip of wind caught us the schooner, full-and-by, with tiller locked, logged 7½ knots for over an hour. Nearing Ecuador that evening, we flashed past a lonely traveller, an orange-and-black snake, deadly-looking, wound disconsolately round a piece of bamboo. A few minutes later a little steamer was seen, heading along-coast. Giving no evidence of seeing us, she presently disappeared under a border-line of mountains to the east. The *Cimba* kept on through the night, breaking a pounding sea, her bows alight with phosphorus. By the next day we found that she had made a run of 125 miles out to windward against a retarding chop and a one-knot head-current, her helm unattended throughout.

The sunset of that day found us under the lofty steps of the Andes, almost on to the bases of crumbling cliffs, under dark gorges arising in a great wilderness to unattainable peaks brushed with clean snow. A play of copper-coloured light lit the heights, falling seaward like a scarlet-and-purple tide. It died out; but as it vanished a promontory just north of Cape San Francisco was sighted. We had gained southing! So, tacking ship, we moved westward over the ocean, to see the Americas no more.

Six hundred miles still separated us from the Galapagos, and before one of these had been covered the wind veered, forcing us on to tacks again. The next day bringing no change, the *Cimba* drove over gaudy waves, with her crew seated on the cabin-top scrubbing clothes beside buckets of rainwater. *From the log of the following night*: "Seas running high. Nimbus clouds on windward horizon. Ship pitching violently in steep-wave formation."

With the tiller locked and the steering-well usually emptied by head-winds, Dombey Dickinson and I would suddenly abandon ourselves to long talks. What would be the perfect cruise? The perfect cruise, we decided, would have to be a cargo-carrying one, for the romance of yachts is not as potent as the romance of working ships. No, the *Cimba* could not be classed a yacht, but, even so, why were we on *this* cruise? I don't think I ever attempted a real answer. To be exact, I don't think I knew how to do so. It was like asking a boy why he liked cake, an old man his pipe. We take what we can get. If there was a sailing merchant marine very likely Dombey and I would be the slaves to some deep-waterman. Why won't one of steam do? Oh, it's not mere nonsense, this insistent mumble of salty voices against the shore-bound invention, the steamer. Nor is it only sentiment, romance. It is something more. A good seaman, to whom all the meaning in the world is wrapped up in his ship, feels a false note in the extravagance of a modern steamer. Strangely enough, he feels that the sailing craft has a utility lacking in her rival. Absurd! Mechanical contraptions are the things of the moment! But is it absurd? Sailing-ships did not have to be

subsidized by Governments or given enormous mail con-
tracts in order to be kept at sea, and one of them could have
made a fortune just by carrying the fuel a steamer burns to
make a single passage. But Sail will return. The steamer is
merely one of many extravagances riding a particular eco-
nomic wave, an expensive gesture of a glorious era, a grand
piece of commercial extravaganza that may be lost for ever
by the falling of another Phoenicia, another Rome, at the
twinkling of an eyelash. And Sail, sound and ageless, will
float back on the first tide that brings simplicity into confusion, calm into chaos. . . . But *why* this cruise? "I've always
liked the idea—pressing in on something new, that we don't
know about," said Dombey, lighting his pipe. "And who
knows what we'll find ahead in it all?" And one of our rare
talks would end, end perhaps lacking the subtlety that was
Carrol's, unfortified by the rich experiences that were Warren's, trailing off into silence, passing away like the pleasant
smoke from Dombey's pipe.

Head-winds clamped down. We would drop the regular
foresail and, fastening the tack of one of the new wingsails to
the foremast foot, hoist it to the main truck, transforming
the *Cimba* into a staysail schooner; or, again, we would set
the wingsail to the fore, and sheet home the clew, acquiring
a jib-headed, free-footed foresail. These new sails, designed
to meet all three purposes, drew well and proved easy to
handle.

Twelve days out we ran into cold weather brought about

by the Humboldt Current. Once more the coal stove was lighted, a hot meal served up that night. Until now we had lived almost entirely on fresh provisions—plantains, bananas, beans, and yuka (a variety of yam)—having broached only half a dozen tins of preserved foods. The squalls increased, and one of us kept to the deck night after night, while the schooner fumed under smoky moonlight, her halyards cleared, but still sailing herself. Once in a while there would come from the deck an excited cry, "Here it is!" And we would rapidly join forces as a squall blasted down and began to overwhelm the lone ton of keel ballast; but only rarely, for we were not often run upon so hard or so quickly that one man couldn't manage the gear. Finally, on the last night out, the *Cimba* crossed the Line, her man on deck bundled in sweater and coat.

The following afternoon an ashen mist, very fine, spread the horizon. The wind, wet and west, pawed at the caps of an ocean icy and rolling in half-hearted sunshine. By and by the haze drew off, dissolved, and two mounds of land were seen towering darkly over the swaying sea—the first islands of the Galapagos, Chatham and Indefatigable, reared in shadow against the skyline. Diving heavily, throwing a lot of spray, we slowly closed in as the sun went down, and the schooner, with helm still untouched, knuckled into a lifting, unshining sea.

The dark, tomb-like islands of the Galapagos, their dead, volcanic bodies separated from one another by wide ranges of ocean, are perhaps best identified by the names of their few anchorages—by Academy Bay on Indefatigable Island, Wreck and Freshwater Bays on Chatham, Tagus Cove on Albemarle, and by Post-office Bay on Charles Island. Four people, perhaps seven, live on Charles, two on Indefatigable, and a handful of peons on Chatham.

Some time in early morning we came abeam Wreck Bay, cleared the lee of Chatham, and bore down on Charles Island, our destination. With the sun back the first hour of fair wind on the entire passage passed with the *Cimba* running at nine knots to bring abeam Champion, a guano island, white and resembling an iceberg, and, finally, Charles Island, gained after sixteen days and fourteen hundred miles of calm and squall.

Under barren heights we brought up, headed inshore, and made a flying moor off the rim of a white-sand beach. The sails dropped, a bird screamed, and from the parched volcanic slopes a silence seemed to gather way, to roll down and close in about us and about the rolling schooner. This was deserted Post-office Bay, where at one time whalers, a year or two from home, would call to find letters brought by outward-bounders in a cask on the edge of the beach—a place I have heard is haunted to this day by the slush lights of old New Bedford ships, by dim figures parading that fine strip of sand, almost lost on a seashore of rotted lava.

We took the tender from the cabin-top, stripped the tarpaulin, set it rigid, and rowed ashore. On the beach we came upon the wreck of a small boat, two skeletons, and the wind-worn footprints of a man. A curious place for a man to come, we thought! The sand ended abruptly where streams of lava had rolled into the bay, while beyond, on three sides, a thicket of dead brush listed far up to the brim of a distant crater. An overgrown path led to a mound of small stones propping up a ship's timber supporting the post-office, a weatherbeaten cask. It was not the original cask, but one erected by the British Scientific Expedition of 1924. Dombey opened a small door hinged to its side by strips of old leather. It was empty.

A few yards farther inland we came upon what must have been a compound, a clearing in the brush. Tracings of road-ways and paths neatly bordered by shells and stones wandered into the brush for a hundred yards or so, then trailed off. Long since they had failed to lead anywhere. But where could they ever have led on this lonely island? Dividing dead brush from dead brush, mysterious stone walls ran the length of the thicket. There were one or two graves. Towards the centre of the clearing a warped flagpole, its halyards gone, pointed forlornly to the sky, and beyond it, in partial ruin, its veranda fallen away, stood a solitary building. Going inside, we found three musty rooms, empty, littered with rusted cooking utensils, German catalogues, old estimates of mining equipment. Learning nothing further, we went back to the clearing, and were about to go into the brush when Dombey exclaimed, "Look there!" By the side of the house was a water-tank in a state of ruin, and on it was painted a crude arrow and the words "Hacienda Paradise." House of Paradise! We looked up the forbidding hills of basalt, partially yellowed with low shrub, for the most part bare and wind-cut, towards which the arrow pointed. So it was somewhere within that unearthly silence that Paradise had been found!

The sun was far down, flashing over the sea, throwing a slight flush upon the island, driving long shadows inland. A crater-top glowed with light, another became sombre and purple, and we, knowing that it was too late to climb the hills that day, went aboard, to return with supplies for supper. Dombey, with a .38, disappeared one way, and I, with a machete, another, each to go over the coast in the descending twilight. We returned at dark with armfuls of wood, made a roaring fire, and cooked a supper of pancakes and tea. We discussed the finds. The footprints and the wreck remained unaccounted for, but some piping and a sluice, together with the mining catalogues, suggested an abandoned hydraulic mine. And yet would a mine account for the neat stone walls or the paths so painstakingly bordered? We racked our minds in vain, neither of us guessing that we were having supper among the ruins of a lost Utopia; that the obscured paths and the partially hidden walling were the physical remains of a dream, of an ideal, attempted by a lonely group of Scandinavians endeavouring to form the perfect, the ultimate, community. The silent roads, the flagpole without a flag, pointed perhaps not so much to the frailties of men as to the frailties in the systems of men. And in the end this Utopia had been left but one purpose: it bore a sign leading to a new one—"Hacienda Paradise."

A COLD WIND sprang off the sea, moaned in the bush, and swung up and over the big island, over silent craters, through wildernesses, and dark, indiscernible valleys. The fire spluttered and grew low, its circle of light smaller. But from all around another circle widened, expanded—the circle of all that is ageless, widening for the infinity beyond the horizons. The twentieth century was lost, left astern. A scream from the forest! And a wild donkey, braying shrilly, thundered past the fire. The lusty wind came on again, a peak of cold moon cut the sea-edge, and we, stamping out the fire, launched the boat and rowed for the resting *Cimba*.

TEN

A GALAPAGAN MYSTERY

A NEAR-BY rifle-shot broke the air at sunrise. Dombey hurried the Winchester on deck and fired in reply. When no answer came the two of us made ready for a march inland. The two stock anchors were given full scope, while doubled bights of line were run from the foremast foot to an old mooring in the bay. The companions were locked; then, taking the repeating rifle, a pistol, a bush knife, a flour-bag of raisins, and a flask of water, we rowed ashore, to discover fresh footprints on the beach. Some one had come out of the thicket, walking with short, almost feminine steps, and had stood for some while facing the schooner before returning into the bush. On losing the tracks inshore it once more occurred to us that Post-office Bay was a curious place to lure a human being.

Obtaining a bearing from the arrow on the water-tank, we walked inland, losing the sea. Stumbling on a dim trail, splashed here and there with the same paint used for the arrow and sign, we ascended a bed of loose lava, black and dry. A mile on and up the sea appeared over-shoulder, a calm expanse run over by waves of light, hot and flashing from the equatorial sun. Far out a kite-shaped thing, a giant ray, flung itself into the light, careened, and fell back to the glaring sea with a large splash; under the heel of the land the *Cimba* swung safely at her hooks. Pressing on, we climbed a deposit of loose stones, winding through a parched valley like a dry stream, eventually gaining an immense plateau, where a range of volcanoes brooded over a sparse, forsaken wilderness. In the melancholy of yellow leaves small birds, the only visible life, fluttered silent and unafraid.

A valley, caught between the upright breasts of two craters, swung off the eastern limit of the plateau, and here, on its shaly reach of withered trees and cactus-stump, we saw tracks of donkeys and wild dogs—the descendants of ships' mascots, which attack like wolf-packs and have to be stopped by gunfire. The tracks were old, most of the life having retreated to the few waterholes on the peaks. Again rifle-shots were heard, and once more answered with the 30.30, to bring the strangers to silence. Several times we lost the trail slanting up the slope of a crater glittering with substratum metals, and then, with the whole mountainside ablaze, we called a halt, broke out the raisins, and drank from the flask. We moved on, and, reaching the crater, saw the land circling beneath us, pensive and desiccated, its shadowless mountains stacked over valleys, the valleys reared in immense waves above the sea. After half circling the crater-lip we swung down, and passed over an arid shoulder of basalt, to find at its base a small oasis of green lemon-trees, shining and blowing in the wind.

With pockets filled with lemons we crossed a mile or so of shale, to enter another valley, silent, ridged by dead lava lifting to the midday haze in dry, perpendicular slopes. Suddenly we stopped. Above on a jagged ledge a figure was crouched, gazing at us, a boy whose hair fell almost to his shoulders, whose sunburned body was bare except for a loin-cloth supporting a long knife in a skin sheath. He was shielding his eyes against the sun, glaring at us with even more amazement than that with which we regarded him.

"Hello!" I said, perhaps too suddenly. He drew back, turned, and began to run. Still crouching, he sprang with the grace of an animal along the ledge, his arms straight down, his back bent forward, disappearing before our eyes like a vision.

"Well, of all the—" exclaimed Dombey.

A bearded man, his hair reaching well down a coarse shirt, was suddenly shaking us by the hand, speaking briskly in some foreign tongue, which sounded like German. He had appeared out of nowhere, a smile on his weathered features, a Mauser rifle in his hand, gesturing that we follow him up the incline.

At the door of the House of Paradise a woman, standing so strangely, so pleasantly, amid the wilderness, greeted us, and, together with the man, urged us into the shelter of grass and driftwood. A little table on the stone paved floor was hurriedly laden with melon, a salad of greens and lemon, as we, like guests of primitive times, were given food the very first thing. Not until afterwards was it discovered that two of us could speak no German, the other two scarcely a word of English; nevertheless, what with gestures, pencil-sketches, stray words, an English-German dictionary, we made considerable headway.

The man, middle-aged, full-bearded, sat before us like a noble scholar in careless garments, a scholar who, instead of being bowed down by a painfully learned philosophy, happily derived his enthusiasms from it. And the woman might just have come in from shopping in a European street. There was a charm and a gentleness about her—nothing of the erratic, of the careless or the unwomanly—and it was easy to see who controlled the slight conventions even a paradise must have. She was—and it must take character to be this in a wilderness—a lady.

They explained to us, their first visitors for over two years, that they asked only ammunition and matches of the outside world, that often they went months without either. Why had they left that world behind? Just in time we remembered that the gracious traveller listens rather than questions. Consequently we waited in vain for a story that was not forthcoming. We told of the rifle-shots about Post-office Bay. Who could it have been? Could it have been the boy seen on the cliff? Heavens, no! *Kleiner Knabe* has no gun; he has a knife. No one goes to the Bay. It is abandoned, the hunting terrible. They talked together a short while, then, still mystified, arose to show us the second of the three rooms, where an eighteen-months-old baby slept in a rude cradle, and then a tiny kitchen beyond it, clean and spare in equipment.

We went outside. A small garden patch, waving in the wind, dipped steeply to a valley—a great depression of rock rolling for the ocean. Here and there within the garden green leaves, the glitter of Life surrounded by Death, were shining in the harsh afternoon light. Suddenly the boy appeared amid them, to stand watching us. The couple, obviously his parents, paid no attention as they showed us over the garden, Only an acre or so in all, it was laid out with Teutonic precision—small plots of corn, wheat, potatoes, and even adequate strips of cotton, coffee, and tobacco. And behind us the boy followed, not closely, but from a distance, his eyes constantly upon us. At the head of the garden we inspected the sides of beef in a smokehouse cut into the sheer cliff, and beside it, to make all this possible, a small spring, trickling as if by magic out of the dead earth.

It was getting late when we went back to the house to give the couple a bundle of magazines and the jars of marmalade carried from the *Cimba*. The woman was delighted by this latter gift, valuing the jars above their contents, but neither of them, asking only ammunition and matches of the world, knew quite what to say to the magazines, printed in English and crowned by gaudy advertisements. In the end they laughed over them—they who showed so little curiosity regarding a new Germany or a post-War world. They had wandered away perhaps to lose all of the world, yet certainly to find a happiness in one of the most unyielding places on earth.

It was nearly time to leave when the boy came and stood silently in the doorway. Lithe and supple, with a body almost as dark as his long hair, he was perhaps sixteen years old. He gazed steadily upon us with a pair of handsome eyes that shifted only if Dombey or I tried to catch them with a glance. There was something untamed, subjective, and yet noble about him all at once. Standing before us was a boy, as close as possible to the hypothetical natural state; erect, tense, fortified by fresh, extremely strong instincts, strange only because of the purity of their state.

The sun fast sinking, we arose to go, declining an invitation to stay the night, and accepting with reluctance a copy of *Galapagos—World's End*. I went up to the silent boy and, smiling, put out my hand. He hesitated a moment, gripped it with a firm clasp, and, putting his feet together, made a courtly bow. He looked up, and I thought I caught a faint smile.

A final sweep of light, cold, brazen, penetrated the valley as we descended. On looking back we saw a triangle of small figures standing under the gloom of an Indian-ink mountain.

"*Auf Wiedersehen!*" called the woman. "*Auf Wiedersehen!*" And she waved encouragingly from her paradise found at the world's end. After all, perhaps both Plato and the Norwegians of the Bay had lost Utopias because the Perfect State cannot exist beyond the family group, beyond the depths of love, which acclaims itself neither as a monarchy nor a democracy, and yet is greater than both. Waving towards the mountain, we turned and marched slowly into the valley.

In dusk, in darkness, in moonlight, we found a way. Some distance on there was a crude obelisk of stones marking the beginning of a trail leading to Black Beach, where the widow of a Dr Ritter lived in seclusion. Too late to think of deviating, we held south under large ashen craters, groped through the thickets, passed the wide plane, at a late hour descending to sea-level to find Post-office Bay windless in cool moonlight.

Before going aboard we stumbled upon something strange. The heavy door of the settlement building, wide open before we left, was now firmly closed. Of weighty oak, it opened inward so stiffly that a half-gale could not have swung it; yet here it was, at the end of a calm day, tightly closed. Forcing it quickly, we hurried inside, not returning until knowing the old building to be empty. There was not another clue. And the moon revealed no further footprints about the clearing or the beach.

We returned to the *Cimba*, our stay on Charles Island over. To our regret we were leaving behind something un-solved—footprints, unexplained gunshots, a mystery of sorts, parts of which have never been satisfactorily explained. But we were in dry islands, using ship's water, with three thousand miles of open ocean ahead. Under the cabin lamp we opened the volume of *Galapagos—World's End* at the fly-leaf, where our friend, the lady at Paradise, had written an inscription. As far as we had known, on going ashore there were but two camps on the island, one belonging to the widow at Black Beach, the other to the notorious Baroness Wagner, whom we thought we had visited that day. But the signature beneath the inscription was not hers at all, but that of some one else. Where in those godforsaken mountains could she be? Could she explain the rifle-fire, the footprints, the closed door at the post? Why had not our friends, who many times mentioned Mrs Ritter, spoken once of this third party?

We learned nothing more, not another thing, and for a long while the world heard nothing of the tragedies of Charles Island. And then came news of the breaking up of the Baroness Wagner's stronghold, of the hill-fighting between her men, of a stranded boat with two skeletons beside it on one of the northern islands, and, finally, of the unexplained disappearance of the Baroness herself— tragedies which, almost unavoidably, came about while we lay at anchors.

From the log. "Got under way at 10 A.M. for Tagus Cove, Albemarle Island, distant 117 miles. Tide-rips off Daylight Point. South-easterly winds light, current favourable."

ELEVEN

A RENDEZVOUS AT THE WORLD'S END

WE SAILED west seventy miles, eased sheets in the moonlight, and stood on under Western Albemarle, under steep and black cliffs charged by breakers leaping with a roar a hundred feet up the rock. In looming shadow great upright washes of sea, phosphorus-filled and whitened by the moon, mounted, glowed brightly, and, in thunderous explosion upon explosion, collapsed into darkness. The *Cimba*, following some two hundred miles of coast, moved quietly all the next day, the sleeping sea under her, the massive form of Albemarle Island high above, grey, uninhabited, of sulphur, alkali, of great ranges of basalt, dropping so steeply at sea-edge that we, hugging the shore, sailed with a thousand fathoms beneath keel. All day long sea-mews planed mast-high over the water, with stiff-winged albatross scouting far above them, occasionally diving to a green sea broken by porpoises and the wake of sluggish sharks.

In the night, which resembled one of a northern autumn, we forereached towards Tagus Cove, the only anchorage of all that coast. As the moon cut the black brim of a sugar-loaf we saw a tall shadow in the cliff-work, an up-and-down entrance in the rock. Standing in under all sail, to depend on a quick rudder rather than sluggish manoeuvres to fend off danger, we observed in the eerie light that the opening looked little more than a few yards in width—a narrow slot, demanding fine steering. On either side rose the stony gates of Tagus Cove, layer upon layer of absolutely vertical basalt towering eight hundred feet into the air, separated not by a few yards at all, but by a full quarter of a mile of dark water. The white *Cimba*, her sails pulling easily, glided into a canyon—an incredible mirage illuminated above us, dusky, in a bas-relief of moonlight. Three-quarters of a mile on the cove ended, and a 4000-foot crater, pitch-black in its mystery, lifted like a titanic backdrop over the scene.

As Dombey and I lined up an anchorage the moon revealed something on the water that had been hidden in shadow—another boat! We let go anchors, fetching bottom in ten fathoms, and, setting up the collapsible skiff, rowed for the stranger, soon recognized as the famous *Svaap*, the American ten-ton ketch, one of the smallest and stoutest of the round-the-worlders.

Two months before the *Svaap*, which had circumnavigated the globe, had been well under way on a second expedition when her owner, William Albert Robinson, who wrote of her in that splendid book *10,000 Leagues over the Sea*, was taken desperately ill with acute peritonitis. When his condition was almost beyond hope Mrs Robinson, a very brave person, signalled a wandering tuna-boat, whose wireless brought a destroyer and seaplanes to the rescue to rush the couple to Panama. Robinson was saved, but ever since the *Svaap* had rolled abandoned amid the silences of Tagus Cove.

We went on board and, striking matches in the cabin, saw the signs of a hurried leavetaking—emptied sail-lockers and chart-racks, remnants of clothing, rusted tins of food scattered on the floorboards.

Leaving Dombey in the cabin, I went on deck and eased myself into the steering-well. What sights can be seen from the helm of a single craft guided by resourceful hands! The sighted green glitter of a southern island bearing over the bows; a foam of breakers heaving to some romantic coast; the heated shore-lines of jungles, calm, steaming; islands of coral, voluptuous islands of flowers, islands of rocks. And yet to the small-boat voyager it is the sea which comes first; it is the supreme consideration, stretching to every shore, wind-cut and passionate, greater in breadth and loneliness than all the deserts of the world together.

It was time to go when Dombey appeared. After over-hauling the ground-tackle and pumping bilges—the *Svaap* had recently been strained in an accident in Ecuador——we went back to the *Cimba* at 2 A.M., turning in to leave the two adventurers rolling in the windless bay, their white sides misty, grey with moonlight, leaving them—one the veteran, the other of the young that for ever champ at their hawsers—to their own communion beneath the precipices.

When we came on deck with our breakfast Tagus Cove resembled a formidable Norwegian fjord. First to catch our eye were the names of previous expeditions printed in white paint on the base of the dark cliffs: the brigantine *St George*, the schooner *Zacu*, and, as I recall, the *Yankee, Pilgrim, White Shadow*—all names of comparatively large vessels. Those of smaller cruisers were strangely lacking. "I guess the big fellows can go in for that sort of thing," remarked Dombey over tea. "More man-power, more energy. They don't get so worn."

Exchanging our cranky tender for the *Svaap*'s cuyuka, we paddled to the extreme head of the cove, to the only landing on the shore. Names of old whalers had been cut into waterworn stone, one dated 1866, another 1833. Climbing the steep sides, we looked over a summit to see a bright crater lake of green, which on descending proved to be salty, and fed evidently by a subterranean passage. Over in another section we followed the dried bed of a stream, hoping to come upon game lured by a possible pool, but although we ascended to the source we found neither water nor a target for our firearms. The sun made us thirsty, and we cut strips of Ecuador cactus, sucked them, and, parting company, climbed the rolling lava. Before we returned to the landing-place Dombey discovered the skeleton of a dog and the tracks of a wild pack, I a curious heap of misplaced granite lying amid volcanic dust. If the inland was barren of life the shore was not. We fished along it, catching large crabs, coming upon both land and water lizards, immense, motionless, black, as well as sea-lions, who, far from showing fear, even charged the cuyuka.

By sunset we were turning in to rest on the eve of our longest passage. But we did not sail on the following day after all. Instead we idled under cliffs, as though hypnotized by something in the extraordinary silence. Tagus Cove was of the long-dead, a gigantic shelter in Gothic hushing out the sound of the sea; a place of little wind, of less sunshine. And so it was not until the third morning that preparations began for a voyage to the South Seas. By noon rigging lanyards had been set up in their deadeyes, lifelines bowsed taut to the stays, the wingsails and their booms overhauled in readiness for favourable wind. Just as we were finishing work something unexpected occurred. After putting a final tuck in a long splice I happened to look along the cliffs towards the silent entrance, to see, directly ahead, a large topsail schooner bearing down. Dombey, working on the lacing about the main boom, also glanced up. What on earth?

There was the scream of an air-whistle, and a flag broke out on the white schooner—the French tricolour of our comrade of the Canal, the *La Korrigane*.

She came on, looking scarcely a tenth of her size under the walls of the cove, and when a cable's length away dropped anchors smartly and rounded-up in man-of-war style. We hurried into the tender and pulled in her direction. Just off the Jacob's ladder the tender foundered, and we had to tow it as we swam for the side. Every one was laughing by the time we reached the steady decks, to be led below to lend our wet presence to a well-appointed saloon, there to tell of the run from Panama and to listen to the accounts of our hosts over cooling, pleasant drinks.

The *La Korrigane's* afterguard was a happy one, made up of Count and Countess Etienne de Ganay, Mr and Mrs Charlie van de Broek d'Obrenan, and Mr John Ratisbonne. They told of faint head-on breezes, of a light-winded passage that tied with our sixteen-day trip, although no doubt some time was lost by the unique procedure of holding a cocktail-party in mid-ocean for the members of a passing steam yacht. It was strangely pleasant—the sound of many voices, those occasional laughs, the tinkle of tableware, the scent of cigarette smoke, the talk of places to the north already less defined, already losing reality.

Abandoning the idea of sailing that day, we joined a fishing-party in a mahogany launch. A mile to the west of Tagus Cove we steered into a small-mouthed grotto in the cliffs, a rough-hewn cave rising fifty feet above us. A shaft of sunlight, penetrating a narrow opening in the dome, lit a circle of echoing water, the rays filtering to the floor beneath, encrusted with orange corals, red sponges—a wavering mosaic of vivid colour shining beneath the boat's propeller.

While trawling the western shore of the cove more black bass, cod, mackerel, and tuna were caught in two hours than we had taken on our entire voyage. Sea-lions were a drawback to our sport, charging the hooked fish, sometimes to part the line, sometimes to snap a big catch in half. We had many a tug-of-war with them, and whenever a lion lost and the catch was safely landed he would let out a grievous roar and charge the motor-boat.

That evening, before going on board the French yacht, we dressed for dinner—that is, we put on shirts for the first time in several days. Over fragrant coffee we learned that while we were fishing the ladies had enthusiastically attacked the shore, Mrs Van den Broek making several excellent sketches of the cove, while her sister-in-law, the Countess de Ganay, gifted with the genuine curiosity of the explorer, covered a remarkably wide range to the eastward. The *La Korrigane* held the happiest group of any large-craft expedition we came upon, and we noted with interest that, besides other favourable factors, her group was a family one; that the yacht was large, the party small, and that every one served some function, from Mrs Van den Broek, engaged in art-work, to her brother, the Count de Ganay, who alone navigated the schooner and supervised the crew of nine Bordeaux seamen.

of the 1st of August th
party promising that v
other side of the Pacific.
for the South Seas with all pos
we, who must wait until the sun cleared t
ountains for a series of bearings, waved them on their way.
Just before leaving their seamen climbed the cliffs and, gaining a perch high above the other ship legends, painted the
name "La Korrigane," and beside it "Cimba," and underneath "1934."

The last echoes from the Frenchman's whistle died out,
and presently, with topsails whitened by sunshine, she disappeared beyond the headland, leaving the *Svaap* and the
Cimba once more alone. "She'll set a record this run," we
prophesied when she had gone.

And now it was time for a final boarding of the *Svaap*,
so, paddling the cuyuka to the side of the old ketch, we
swung it on board and lashed it to her trunking. For a moment we stood upon the dry deck, feeling that air of faith-
fulness, of loyalty, pervading all good and hard-tried ships.
I recalled that Edward Turpin, a dear friend, an admirable
sailor, and the first with whom I planned our voyage, often
spoke of the *Svaap* as the perfect cruiser; that later, when
we were studying various hulls, Carrol spoke so highly of the
sanity of her lines, of her strength. We tidied her rigging,
paid out more chain, made sure that the cabins were ventilated against dry-rot, and finally pumped her dry. No more
could be done. We threw a few rusty tins of meat into the

g with our water-butt filled from the ta.
. the *Cimba*.
a while it looked as though we should be hela
ed; then shortly after noon, when a thin draught of a
ept the cliffs, we swung the dry canvas aloft, tripped anchor, and began to move. The distance between the two
boats grew greater. Near the entrance we looked back to see
the *Svaap* for the last time, a small form, chalk-white and
rolling easily in the everlasting shadow. Then we lost her,
and, fetching the mouth of Tagus Cove, slipped out to a
sunny sea dancing in wind.

While passing towards the ocean late that afternoon we
ran close on to Narborough Island, and sighted the wreck
of a black-painted vessel some sixty feet long. Unable to
force a landing, we looked closely for signs of life, and fired
shots to draw attention. Not a soul appeared, the island
seemed deserted, and finally we worked the *Cimba* clear and
stood off for the sea.

In the evening dew fell under a waning moon, and there
came the sound of whales from somewhere on the ocean. All
that night we lay becalmed, but morning brought a stir of
wind, and we took departure from a point under the mountain of Narborough. There was no sign of the *La Korrigane*
as we dipped to the west. The volcanoes of the Galapagos,
cryptic and mystic, faded from sight like worn-out bodies of
land, like enchanted dust-heaps floating beneath the sky.
And somehow we were glad they were astern.

TWELVE

THE DOWNHILL RUN

IT WAS DURING the afternoon of the 2nd of August that the Galapagos were dropped and the *Cimba* began a three-thousand-mile run for the Marquesas Islands, far down the South Seas; began with the trade winds yet some distance away, with the swell gentle, the breezes head-on and sweeping out of a murky sea-fret colouring the horizon.

As far as was known, the best time over this more or less popular passage was that of twenty-three days, made by a large schooner yacht, a record we prophesied the *La Korrigane* would break if she pulled decent winds. But long ago we decided that the *Cimba*, the smallest to attempt the crossing, could also make a fair showing; not a better one, perhaps, but one almost as good as that of larger craft. And it was with this very much in mind that we entered the routine of the voyage.

The idea of a cruising vessel racing against time rather than running easily to the South Seas is not a strange one. To show a craft in her best light, to use efficiently all of her incessant effort over water, brings to the crew of racer or cruiser a more healthy discipline, smarter seamanship. In this case it was hardly presumptuous of us to attempt to approach the time of the big schooner, for large vessels rarely find enough wind over this area, while the *Cimba*, underrigged though she was, had an unusual ability to plane behind the kick of moderate waves. Further, to drive her was no harder than letting her lag; every sail was inboard, easy to handle, snug; the arduous spirit of the ocean racer was there, the difficult, backbreaking work missing.

But whatever hopes we held seemed doomed to end at the very beginning. We could not draw the favourable trades, and for most of the important first week worked the rolling schooner through calms and head-winds, stealing only a little longitude over the wide curve of ocean. With dismay we noted the growth of weed along the water-line, choking the overloaded hull in the waning winds of August. A passage of forty days, not twenty-three, appeared the best that we could expect.

Then one night we saw the last of the moon, to be left hanging over a stilled darkness until morning, when, quite suddenly, draughts of wind struck the port quarter from the east-south-east. They held direction, slowly increased, pushed booms against backstays, and brought us into the Trade Belt, five hundred miles from the Galapagos.

The south-east trade winds, waning with the season, were not ever-constant. They veered south and stiffened, backed east and lightened, blew with some vigour at dawn, only to diminish before noon, to lie low until early night, when they might tighten and hold before becoming the ghosts of the middle watch. Sometimes stray squalls would break them up; sometimes they disappeared entirely, perhaps to give way to the short-lived head-winds, which were in turn conquered by the eventual return of southerly draughts. Nevertheless the weather, which had been dull, cold, and overcast, gave way to strong sunshine, and it was as though a dark spring was over and summer beginning.

With the trades more or less aft, the foresail was dropped, and one of the wingsails, sheeted home to its red-painted boom, was ballooned over the bow. For all the pull to these sails they could not be hung out together without dowsing the mainsail, and as that was an impracticable move the *Cimba* carried but two sails, one on the fore and one on the main.

In the first four days of wind she logged 147, 158, 170, and 141 miles.

To us this was excellent work, but we knew that to approach the time of the large yacht she would have to *average* more than 140 miles a day out to the Marquesas; that she would have to be very constant during the more aimless hours, and make the real time in the first five hours after sunrise and in the first five after dark; all of which sounded very fine and extremely improbable.

The days of self-steering were over; only for seconds at a time did the helm go unattended as we lengthened the wheel tricks. The watch came on in the morning, carrying his breakfast to the steering-well. At noon his lunch was handed up, and he remained in the well until six in the evening, when, after twelve hours at the helm, he was relieved by the other man. At midnight the man who had been on all day took the tiller again, tending ship until six, then to be relieved after eighteen hours of duty in twenty-four. Now, apart from a few chores, he was free throughout the day, justifying, we thought, the watch system in the *Cimba*. Experiments in reversing the procedure, giving a long watch below at night, were unsuccessful. To the helmsman, sunrise to sunset seemed shorter than sunset to sunrise, while neither of us found trouble in sleeping night or day.

A typical day while running down the south-east trades:

At six o'clock sharp the man about to take over is roused from the swaying bunk, perhaps by the bell overhead, possibly by the helmsman, sleepy-eyed and powdered by a thin coating of salt taken on in the night, shaking him by the shoulder. "Turn out! Turn out! Time's up!" or "Rise and shine on the workhouse line!" As usual it has been cool enough to sleep fully clothed under the blanket that the man now casts aside. The cabin is still not fully lighted, although fresh shafts of sunlight dip through the ports, and a running pattern of water-light plays on the overhead. With an effort he jumps up, goes to the roaring Spanish stove, and pours some tea into a large tin cup. The tea is strong, and, taking the cup and a handful of ship biscuits, dry or with marmalade, he makes a studied way aloft, joining the helmsman, who somehow looks as though he had held the deck since the beginning of the voyage.

"How has it been?" the newcomer asks.

"Middling. Easy from two on, and freshened at dawn."

"What average?"

"About five and a half. Well, take it—west by south."

"West by south; all mine."

Left alone, the man holds the tiller in one hand, the teacup in the other. He is not fully awake, and sniffs deeply at the pungent salt, always strongest at this hour; sniffs also at other odours, of damp paint wetted by night dew, of saturated cordage and sailcloth. But the fragrance of the tea is supreme, and he holds it near while his eyes leave the compass, take in the schooner, then wander over the ocean, which is gleaming, sharp-cut, a blue glow lifting with the light, and so fresh that it is as though creation had taken place a moment before. Over-shoulder the sun, which had been red and heavy, expands and begins circling the sea. Grey horizon clouds break up, turn white, and start across the sky. The day is well under way. The new helmsman sets his tea-cup aside, perches on the weather rim of the steering-well—which happens to be the port side—and, adjusting the foot-brace within the well to meet the angle of the diving craft, settles down to the task before him.

By ten o'clock the sun is overhead, the helmsman beginning to feel its heat. Off come jacket and shirt, to leave his body, almost native-colour from many watches, protected only by shorts or a pair of cut-down dungarees. He wears no cap, but, leaning overside, wets a large towel and winds it about his head like a turban, arranging it so that a dangling tail protects the nape of his neck. Every so often he clamps the tiller in the comb to pour a bucket of cool sea-water over himself, then several more upon the steaming decks. The white of the cabin-tops and the raised foredeck he wets thoroughly, but the buff-coloured waterways and after-deck are the main consideration: they are possibly ten degrees warmer than the white surfaces, and sting the soles of his bare feet.

And now all ropes, contracted by the moisture of the night, begin to slack off. They must be taken up, but not carelessly and all at once, lest the sail-roping be stretched and the sails lose shape and set. So the helmsman unties the man-rope hitched to his waist and carefully overhauls all working halyards, the wing boom-brace, the preventer, even

the lifelines drooping along the stays. Only the rigging lanyards of Italian hemp, more or less impervious to the night,
he leaves alone. Returning to the well, he fastens the man-
rope about his waist; but no sooner has this precaution been
taken than the wind shifts a quarter-point. He eases the
main sheet, goes forward, and adjusts the wingsail. Again
he over-hauls the halyards, and secures them to pins with
by-the-wind hitches, coiling the running parts with the sun,
faking them down on the cabin-tops. At the tiller once
more, he looks for wind changes over what seem to be two
distinct oceans—one the area to starboard and off the bows,
away from the sun, which is gay, deeply blue, sharply defined, and the other to port and astern, sunward, which is
not blue at all, but only a harsh glare of waves rising and
rolling, sun-lighted, heated, wind-blown. There is no change
in sight, so, lowering his eyes, he gives attention to the black
diamond point on an already yellowing compass-card; he regards it gravely, with the gaze of a seer into a crystal. West by
south . . . west by south. Surely he is in a trance as he leans
unblinking over the little glass instrument, his body wiry,
dark, his white turban nodding ever so slightly. But, no—
suddenly he looks to the weather sea, his glance slowly circling the points of wind effort until gaining the bows. There
the hollowed scoop of wingsail is ballooning, apparently
pulling like a team of horses, responsible for all those vicious
lunges of the bows. But he is not deceived, and looks almost
affectionately at the mainsail, that small conservative spread

that is accounting for six of the eight knots. From compass to sea, from sea to sails, his eyes wander untiringly as all the while he keeps balance, eternally adjusting his back to the changing angles of the deck; not to the slow slanting of a big vessel, but to the lightning-quick dives, the rapid pitches, of a lively schooner smoking her way westward—a clean-cut white sail lost in blue sunlight. Her stern sinks; the furious little bow slashes, noses, lifts; drops, and the stern raises high: Do or die!

The scene changes as the sun reaches zenith, for, as usual, the trades have eased considerably, and the sea is looser, less blue. It is time for the noon sight (always taken by Dombey, always well taken), and we are together on deck. Although that line trailing over the stern is not a log-line, but a trawl which has yet to hook a fish, we have definite opinions on the day's run. Time has helped us to gauge distances, the reckonings of which we pass between us, watch to watch, until the noon hour, when, after allowing for drift, they are added together and compared against solar observations. With practice this system has become more satisfactory than the results from two patent logs, now discarded, and on the present passage we had yet to be more than two or three miles out. So as the sun steepens one of us estimates the distance run from the last noon at one hundred and thirty-eight miles, the other at a mile or so more. The sun is taken, and then after a short interval we learn that actually one hundred and forty-one miles have been put behind.

The helmsman stays at his post unrelieved, the man below handing up the lunch before disappearing for the afternoon. There are several tough planks of the eternal ship's biscuit, a little salmon, but today, instead of tea or cocoa, there is only the daily ration of lime-juice and water, somewhat sugared, a sea tonic of old with a citric tang, giving the illusion of a cool drink. The meal over, he dowses the tinware in the wake, then puts it by until going off watch. He observes that all at once the golden-clear weather has given place to a diffused glare, that the sea is moving in slower rhythms. This is not necessarily a bad omen, for it happens almost every day. The trades are now dragging over the wave-tops in puffs; but then they are always made up of puffs even at their strongest, when the variations are almost indiscernible, for, correctly speaking, there are no steady trade winds.

His back still sways as though he were riding a swing, and the tiller feels hot in his palms. The schooner forges over the sea, slower now, her masts moving pendulum-like, with the precision and the majesty of a big ship's spars. An hour of lassitude is setting in, affecting the wind, the sleepy sea, the sails, and the helmsman himself. He is in a warmed loneliness, feeling an outreaching isolation without distaste, without conscious revolt. In the idle moment he hears the voices of the Shore: "Isn't the monotony great?" In one of the lockers of the well lies a book (for some reading was done at the helm while in the Caribbean). It is a good tale, and yet it has not been opened. Perhaps monotony is what one makes it; perhaps there is no monotony in the real sense at sea—no boredom, at least. "You should have a radio"—the voices again. But somehow there is no desire for a wireless, no craving to be further amused, no desire at all to be in touch with that which was intentionally left behind.

The sun makes westing, and the scene again changes. It is softer now, and somehow the sea looks cooler, almost cold where the lips of the waves spit white in the cloud shadows of navy marching down-sea. The shade from the canvas begins to slant aft over the buff decks, darkening one rail, one track of wash. Suddenly the wind veers two points, and the watch hand-over-hands the main sheet, then jumps forward to tend the wing. Before he returns it has veered yet more, and sails are further sweated in. Half an hour passes, and then the schooner, still struggling with cat's-paws, is on a beam wind, her wing no longer of any use. How can she be helped? The man notches the tiller, goes forward, takes in the sail, sets jib, raises the wing to the mainmast cap, secures its tack to the foremast foot, and sheets home.

Now he handles a craft suddenly converted into a staysail schooner, but, still unsatisfied, breaks out the fisherman staysail, seldom used. He is not content; more can be done, for the jib is not up to the mark at all. He begins some complicated work in the bows, interrupting it ever so often to adjust the tiller, guarding himself from a false step or a stumble as he goes. Soon one of the wingsail poles has been run

out over the bows to serve as a long jury bowsprit, fastened
at the bitter end to the foremast, bowsed against the jib-
stay, and guyed by a pair of lines leading from its cap to the
chain-plates. Upon this contrivance he sets the second wingsail, sheets it far aft, and returns triumphantly to the tiller, to
tend a staysail schooner, now equipped with a bowsprit and
a stout Genoa jib.

Ten miles on, and the wind backs to its old position, the
sail-spread collapses, the jackass rig is taken in, and the wing
put in its former position. With his hands smarting just a little from pulley-hauling on salted line, the helmsman re-
clines, still swaying, in the steering-well, his eyes on the
compass. The sun flashes on the sea, and the watch, for the
first time remembering the sun-glasses in one of the lockers, takes them out and puts them on. As usual they are not
satisfactory while under way, and are shortly abandoned in
favour of a straw hat bought in Porto Bello and now replacing the turban. The wind drops, and the sound of a thousand breaking waves comes in more clearly, to be answered
from on board by the occasional thud of the striving bow, by
the cough of a block.

Two hours pass, and the sun is feeling for the horizon. For
quite a while the wind has drawn off beneath the water-
painted sky, leaving the sea old, affable, and also painted. No
longer is there noise, either from the ocean or the ship, still
gliding for all she is worth, silent and intent. Finally the sun
fetches the horizon; masses of colour begin to burn over the

masts, and the helmsman, looking at a cheap watch kept in the well, sees that it is six o'clock. Going to the companion, he calls down this important fact. Startled by hearing another human voice, he smells the odour of cooking food, and goes back to the tiller. Although his trick is really over, he will have a last twenty minutes on deck, holding a sort of dog-watch, while the relief has his meal in comfort. He sees the sun dip under the skyline, brightening the clouds for a last time. Then the colours fade, and soon the schooner is moving through twilight. He feels something cool strike his back, and turns to discover long fingers of wind moving rapidly over water, dark and ruffled. The sails fill; the schooner pushes on, her decks, only a matter of inches above sea, shuffling water. In no time at all the wake is boiling, and the helmsman must heave on a rigid tiller. Presently he takes the short oaken extension and sockets it over the tiller-head to get more leverage. The tropic twilight, a mood of only a moment, gives in to darkness; the freshening trades shift a quarter-point, and he goes forward to adjust the wing. By now the white housing underfoot has turned dingy, and the sea sweeps to the horizons in one dark shadow. As he leans over the lifelines, feeling for the brace, he thinks for the first time that day how small, how fragile, is the slanting hull— the only object that could float him within a thousand miles. Why, in the dusk even these seas appear ready to overwhelm it! This of all hours is the one that touches his sense of mortality, when the wind, acquiring an almost melodramatic quality, drives coldly against him, tries to press him back to dimmed, half-forgotten states of superstition—the one hour that, regardless of how long he has sailed, he never quite takes for granted. Trimming the wing, he passes cautiously back to the well, now occupied by a dark figure nursing an after-supper pipe. The relief has turned up. After a word or two the man takes his tin plate, cup, and jacket and goes below.

Twelve hours and twenty minutes ago, the time he was last in the cabin, the little Swedish stove was hissing away in its asbestos niche just as it is now. Seating himself before it, he fills his cup with hot cocoa, and finds another handful of ship's biscuit. But his meal is not the sketchy affair of the previous ones, for there is a stew of beef, onions, and potatoes, enough for two men, and to end with, half a tin of Singapore pineapple. As there is no such thing as a mess table in very small ocean schooners he sits on the seat opposite the bunk, and, holding the plate in his lap, continues to sway to the rhythms of the craft. When finished he takes the mess gear to the companion, and, without putting foot on deck, reaches far over and douses them in the sea, now black.

There are a few entries to be made in the logbook, a journal to be brought up to date. Cutting strips of British Navy tobacco, he loads and lights his faithful pipe. Trimming the old-time lamp from the barque *Dorothea*, he writes the story of the past twelve hours, rather hurriedly, with extreme economy, alluding to winds by numerals, to seas and courses by initials and abbreviations. Putting all this away, he glances at the chart, and, crouching over, adjusts lengthwise a board which changes the bunk into a comfortable oblong box. Pulling on a shirt, he climbs in and, feeling chilly, draws up a blanket. And now to sleep—but, no, only to read after all. Fumbling in the bunk, he finds his book, with its two marks showing each man's place, and presently, as the schooner gets under way on one of her five-hour spurts, he wanders from her fighting, which goes on and on, to the supreme luxury of printed pages.

Offshore he cannot read of the sea itself, not even as written of by his secret patron saint, Joseph Conrad. Nor, on the other hand, can he read literature drab in contrast with the clean, majestic action of the sea. No, these days he wants to hear of nobility, of decent love, or of gentleness, and the humble Dickens will charm him as well as any. The book he now reads happens to be Scott's *Kenilworth*, and he is satisfied by its clearly defined heroes and villains. A noise resembling several storms roaring at once rumbles under the bilges; the bows pound vigorously, triumphantly; the bunk lurches, lists, pitches. . . .

> It was thus he avoided Warwick, within whose Castle (that fairest monument of ancient and chivalrous splendour which yet remains uninjured by time) Elizabeth had passed the previous night. . . .

Quite suddenly the bell sounds—and he awakes. Midnight already! Half asleep, he feels for the bell-clapper over the eastern skyline. The watch looks on dispassionately. He is thankful for the dawn, but its arrival does not move him as did the twilight; in fact, in contrast to that hour, this is the time he becomes most careless, the hour during which he is most likely to take an unnecessary chance. The light increases, and, wet through, he locks the idle helm, stands up, yawns, stretches himself, stamps his bare feet, His throat, his nostrils, feel stiff with salt. Walking aft, he pulls at the trolling-line, sees the empty lure skip water far astern, then turns and, with hands on hip, regards the schooner. She is still working on the beam airs, still pressing the issue. Why doesn't she stop, for once! With a yellow haze brightening in the east, the man ends his reverie, looks at the time, and goes below. The other is sleeping soundly, oblivious of all that has happened since midnight, for on this passage the off man is never roused to handle sail. Taking a match from a waterproof tin, the watchman lights the stove, fills the kettle, and sets it to boil. The noise he makes does not disturb the other. Going on deck, he finds a great change. The sea has become almost blue, the sky cloudless, the schooner white, while the sun, just cutting the horizon, is shining on the wet uppers of the sails. Remembering the binnacle light, he dowses it, takes off sou'wester and coat, steers ship until, ten minutes later, on looking at the watch, he goes below, shakes the other, and says, "Time's up!" Reaching deck, he hurriedly strips to the waist, throws the clothes down the hatch, pulls a mop out of the lazarette, and begins splash-

the bunk, striking an answer before turning up the wick and going to the stove for the hot tea the helmsman had jumped down to boil. Before sipping the tea he turns the lamp low, that his eyes will be ready for the deck. The cup empty, he buttons his collar, puts a piece of ginger in his mouth, and, feeling the wind of the deck, appears as a welcome apparition to the helmsman, who would be quite ready to converse if he didn't know that the last thing the twelve-to-six man is capable of is talk. Handing over the woollen windbreaker and a stocking cap, the departing man states the course briefly and makes for the cabin.

The new watch usually begins by scooping up sea-water to wet his face, then inspecting the trim of the sails and the promise in the weather sky. The bow waves are coughing loudly at the time, for the sea is wilder than it was during the day. The sails scud like black wings against the stars as the helmsman, knowing that the trades have held unusually long, thinks it time something happened.

Steadying at course, he reaches inside the binnacle at the extreme end of the after-cabin, turns off the little lamp, climbs on to the cabin-top, and, facing aft, steers from stars astern, from Cleopatra's Stairs, and from one star whose name he does not know, steering a truer course than if he used those forward, which time and again are blotted out by rolling sails. For an hour or more no change overtakes the unlighted schooner, whose running lights, except when in traffic, are kept below to save fuel. But at last the helmsman grows restless, and, making fast the helm, climbs below, returning with a 'night lunch,' a surplus of provisions set aside for the slow-moving ages of the graveyard watch. He is just finishing the sardines and biscuit when the wind, which has held overlong, drops suddenly. The sea becomes noisier than ever, the wind slacks yet more, and for two hours nothing happens, nothing at all.

The clouds climb, hiding the stars. A minute after the binnacle has been relighted a heavy rain begins to fall. There is a cry of wind; the sails are hurled out stiff, and the helmsman goes forward to make sure that lines are clear for running, feeling over-deck cautiously, ever on guard against the false move that may spill him. There is an exciting moment as the wing, wet and straining overside, drives its boom into a fast-pacing sea; then the blow loses force, wanders off into space, and the craft labours quite slowly in the rain. The helmsman sighs, takes a sponge, and attempts to wipe his face, no longer salted, and to clear the binnacle deadlight as well. His eyes smarting somewhat from the glare, he opens the binnacle and fixes a piece of cardboard, crudely slotted to show only a narrow arc of the compass, over the light. There appears to be no wind, but, looking closely, he sees that the schooner is making three knots—on her reputation. He exchanges his cap for a sou'wester, kept in one of the lockers. A hasty glance at the watch shows that it is four o'clock. Two hours to go! Shivering slightly in the downpour, he philosophically takes a pinch of Copenhagen, a dark snuff, and fixes his gaze on the watery deadlight.

It is an hour and a half later, and there is no change, except that the wingsail is missing and the foresail and jib are aloft, striving in the darkness. The rain, which drew off twenty minutes before, is again falling about the wet, almost windless schooner. The watchman has been kept on his feet by light airs playing from point to point. He was forced to furl the wingsail, and once, during a heavy roll, missed a lifeline in the dark, and was compelled to feel out for a shroud. And now, while the regular sail-spread is stretching to a faint beam wind, he once more leans over the compass and mothers the craft westward. Rather hazily he considers the width of this ocean. Maps and charts make for a sort of sophisticated regard for the wide spaces of the earth, until an entire ocean may be visualized as a few inches of blue ink on the surface of a map. For the sake of argument, muses the helmsman, scale down distance from miles to feet, and on this particular passage the schooner will be seen as but a grain of dust blown slowly over a half-mile plane, a fleck of dust that can cover little more than a hundred feet from sunrise to sunrise.

The rain is stopping—and what is this? The binnacle lamp is becoming dim, and a colourless light is rising all around. Slowly out of the darkness grow the familiar outlines of cabin-tops, decks, masts—colourless, blank, grey-appearing, like the forms in a misted photograph. The clouds are parting, are gone, and loose, undeveloped waves also take on grey as a gloomy bar of light comes to float on

ing bucketful after bucketful of sea-water on to trunking and decks, leaving the schooner, which is still talking to the sea, to move for herself. Several flying-fish, lured by lighted port-holes, lie on deck amid a school of minnows, shipped in one of the heeling squalls. When the mop has made the white-and-yellow paintwork shine in the sun he lays it on the gallows frame to dry, and sets about coiling down lines of all descriptions. Presently there is a sound from the hatch, and he sees the relief coming up bearing tea and biscuits and heading for the steering-well. He joins him.

"How was it?" the newcomer asks, staring at the horizon. He seems profoundly amazed, incredulous, at something out there. He is sleepy.

"Broken up. She's lucky if she ran three and a half. But, see—there's a nice little wind making in the south."

At this the relief wakes up. "Good! There's some herring below for you."

"All right. West by south."

"West by south; all mine."

And the watch, after welcoming the new wind slanting over a fresh sea, disappears down the companion.

WORKING WEST and south, we drove, day after day, out to the midway area of our track, and began closing in upon the distant islands. The winds neither increased nor grew steadier, and the *Cimba* strove hard for her daily runs. Once, for a night and part of a day, she was almost becalmed, then pulled a wind, and made the second and last 170-mile run. Her speed continued to drop after midnight and after noon, and she continued to rush through sunsets and sunrises. Her crew learned several things. For example, that in small cruisers long passages are the happy passages, where the crew settle down to a lengthy stretch, responding with some perfection to the rhythms of the ocean, the constant motions of a ship. We learned that life was kept full by the schooner herself. We never spoke of her by name, but always as 'she' or 'her,' and we never spoke of her affectionately. At times she maddened us, at times she interested us by her repertoire of tricks, and then again she would amuse us by sporting gestures, stubborn and all her own. She had a kind of humble gallantry, and she was heroic—but only as simple fishing-folk are heroic.

Swinging through a series of 125-mile days of fluky trades, the *Cimba* ran up these successive runs, with almost steamboat regularity: 141, 167, 148, 146, 149, 148 miles.

And now, despite the increased marine growth on the undersides and the low force of the wind, it looked as though the schooner, if her luck held, was at least going to equal the twenty-three-day run of the large yacht. Perhaps she had that luck. The speed lay in the lines of the hull, but the luck might well be her sails, cut from the bolts of the great Lunenburger *Bluenose*, a charmed fisherman, a fortunate ship, famous for her speed. From dawn to dark her two or three triangles swung over the sea, bellied before the trade, drooped in the variables.

A typical entry from my journal:

Latitude 6° 55′ S., Longitude 118° 53′ W. Strong trade from sunrise on, blowing hard, turning the sea near black. Squalls from S.E. before noon, killing trade. . . . Bunted wingsail and set foresail as wind hauls aft at noon—no go—wind shifts, and we shift again. To-night: squalls, lightning, and confused sea.

With runs of 169, 151, 147, 147, and 146 miles, the *Cimba* reached for landfall. Then, in something of a spurt, she covered the last miles of open water to make landfall off Ua Huka, of the Marquesas Islands, nineteen days from the Galapagos, having averaged 6.4 knots, or 150 miles a day, through thick and thin, through calm and trade, head-weather and fair squalls. There had been no days of particularly favouring weather, and not once were there eight hours of steady wind. A happy trip, almost a remarkable trip—and yet we, the crew, knew how small had been our contribution towards it. We were not deceived; whatever credit was due went directly to the schooner herself, and from there, we trust, to reflect in some degree the honest skill of her lovable builder, Vernon Langille.

We raised the mountains of Nuka Hiva, bore in to Tai-o-hae Bay, and dropped anchors off the village. The sails fell on to salted decks, leaving the bare masts curiously naked and useless. Mystical scents, warm, tropical, came off-shore as we felt something leaving us, weak, awkward, slightly breathless. Even as we gazed at the green mountains, at the shining coco-trees, we knew that it was only that another voyage had ended.

THIRTEEN

IN FRENCH OCEANIA

UNDER THE mountains the bay of Tai-o-hae curved for eleven miles, the village of less than fifty huts almost lost on its arc. A heavy vegetation rose beyond the fringing reef, ascending to the mountains. On all the island, which was large, there were but three white men—the French Resident, who granted us *pratique*, a lonely planter, and Père Simeon, a kind, very elderly priest. We landed on the shore, to find a road under a tight roof of vegetation following the beach. Natives straggled past, dark-skinned, dark-eyed, in bright, brief clothing. They made little of us. Some smiled and said, "*Caoha!*"—a half-familiar word. Of course! "*Aloha!*"—the greeting of another Polynesian people. And some did not speak, and we, with Melville's *Typee* and Stevenson's essays in mind, were a little astonished. What had happened? The high-spirited Islanders of Melville, the less hostile ones of Stevenson, laughter, the garlands, the feasts to welcome the northern transgressors—where were they? The people and the land itself hinted of weariness, of a Far Eastern lethargy, and the road, twisting through wildflower-trees, was an almost empty one. On a mountain trail, where we stopped to pick mummy apples, a group of natives riding bareback on island ponies passed like phantoms, each uttering the word "*Caoha!*" as they moved slowly by in single file. "*Caoha!*"—and no more. The lash on a sweating flank, the noise of hoofs pounding in brush, and into the twilight of the woods the band disappeared like a caravan of the long-dead.

We returned to the bay, and before going on board saw the trading shack of Donald Establishments, of Tahiti, a whitewashed dispensary, the ghost of a gaol, and the Resident's house. Gaining the *Cimba*, lonely in the bay, we brought the stove on deck to cook a supper of fish, plantain, and taro, a purple potato-like vegetable obtained from the natives in trade for scraps of clothing. The sun went down as the meal drew to an end, and presently we sat cleanly shaven in the darkness, smoking East Indian tobacco, occasionally breaking the quiet to talk of the strange disappearance of the proud Marquesan, the fearless Islander. As had many Americans before us, we unhesitatingly blamed the French—blamed them for bringing indentured Chinese, who in turn brought leprosy and plague to wipe out whole villages, as well as for the introduction of smallpox and the tuberculosis that had left Tai-o-hae a ghost village, inhabited for the most part by people of other islands. A great race had fallen to the acquisitive lust of the North, succumbed to its marshalled commercialism, which is seldom better than it has to be, succumbed particularly to the French—at least, so we thought, ignorant that Peruvians, not the popularly criticized French, brought smallpox, that it was an American who marooned a sailor in the last stages of tuberculosis on Fatu Hiva, and another American who was responsible for importing the diseased Chinese labour. And yet it seems that the Marquesas did not fall before the malice of any particular individuals or Governments, but rather were dissolved away before a great system that must have power before the reaction of philanthropy can set in, wealth before dignity, heaped warehouses before nobility; a system touching not only here, but penetrating almost every square mile of a once more contented tropics.

Something bumped the side, and a soft voice called in the darkness. We arose to find an old man of seventy years or more manning a bread-fruit dugout. I recognized him as one who had become attached to Dombey, a genial old native who paddled his canoe with the vigour of a boy. He was imparting news, repeating one word over and over again, persistently and with enthusiasm. Finally we made out that there was a dance on the shore. The band of riders headed for Tai-o-hae was explained, and the silence of the bay was to be broken after all. We climbed into the dugout. The old man paddled for the shore, fixed with the single red eye of a bearing-light perched low and to the right of the invisible village. The moon cleared the dark mountains to fire the water, the old man steadied ship on a swell, and we dived in, making a good landing on the sand.

At a place on the shore where the palms rose high over a narrow circle of grass a group of natives had gathered with their children and their dogs. The moon had yet to lighten the place, and we could only hear the voices of the people, perhaps fifty in all, mixed with the sound of close-by waves, the barking of dogs. The voices were low, husky, happy, high-spirited, childlike, barbaric—laughing amid a wind, damp, salty, and sweet, with the scent of flower forests. Just then the laughter died and a single drum-beat sounded.

Two lighted torches of palm-leaves, held aloft by young boys, threw red and windy flares into the blackness. We moved to the edge of the clearing as a dozen young men with flowered *pareus* about their waists came out of no-where, forming two rows, their backs to the sea, their eyes to the land. A murmur arose from the spectators, a murmur that increased when six girls, their bodies oiled, the flowers in their hair and about their breasts red in the torchlight, made a third row between the men. Not all the girls had the physical beauty accredited by legend, but two of them had; another that timorous form of beauty transmutable by the eyes alone; one had on too much coconut-oil, another's hair was inferior to the waist-long tresses of the group, while two were thick-limbed, broad-browed, square-faced, with high cheek-bones and black, attractive almond eyes.

There was another drum-beat, and once more the laughter stopped as the dancers, losing every trace of self-consciousness, grew tense and frowned in anticipation. In absolute silence they poised their bodies for the drum. Then a dog barked, a wave of laughter surged through the spectators, and the dancers relaxed, smiling enigmatically. A young girl giggled loudly, an old bearded native, lying on the ground, shrieked with laughter, and the night wind thundered in the trees.

The drum again—fast, rhythmical clacking of wood on wood—and the dancers came to life, oily, swaying, as the stage narrowed and the audience was forgotten. The shining forms moved in waves to the brusque sound, until they swayed as one, until they felt the first mood of the dance. Then the drum stopped. But quickly it came back, and the dancers, cut out of blackness by the torches, moved once more. Again the check, and the figures, with arms down, heads bowed, awaited the return of the life-giving drum. A leader suddenly appeared out of the darkness, his face painted, his *pareu* fixed in a bizarre fashion; savage to the point of being comical, he appeared to be aping his warlike ancestors. This, however, could not be, for the group regarded the pantomime almost reverently. He was the leader, creating a charm for dancers. The wood drum boomed, he took up a position in the rear, and the figures responded with dilated eyes and nostrils, with corded muscles and up-flung heads. Suddenly the mountain shadows fell away, the crimson flowers of the dancers turned white, and moonlight had fallen; the palms tossed, the silver sliding on their leaves, while beneath them, as the torches were hurled into the sea, dingy lemon vistas opened out of the darkness.

Now the men throw imaginary spears in the moonlight, grip invisible war-clubs, for a moment becoming the true, the fearless, sons of their fathers. But the heroic has been conquered, has been taught to trade coconuts for the soap-bars and vanilla cakes from beyond the equator, and the stone gods of honour, pride, and bravery are left crumbling in mountain caves. Only love is left. The men fall to the grass, and the girls—the slim, the heavy, the graceful, alike—move in the dance of lovers. The grass waist-pieces sway gently, brown arms scented with oil feel out from dark bodies, hands wave in rippling rows, and as a murmur sweeps through the spectators and grows the drum comes in faster, more demandingly. The fallen warriors rise, surround the girls, and whatever was dream-like in the dance disappears as a sardonic chant, ironically enough to the tune of a Scottish Presbyterian mission hymn, sensuous, black as midnight, rises exultantly. The mad 'Pig Dance' is under way—the dance of the *bourgeois*, of freed people, freed for ever of their noble rulers, their bravest gods. And now, out beyond the dancers, the children giggle, while the old native, flat on his back, stops chanting and once more screams with laughter. But even here is a study in selflessness, for the leader keeps to the rear, and should the drum stop midway the dancers would be left as breathless rows of idols, identical in the moonlight. The chant grows; the figures move convulsively; bodies, arms, veneered with oil, flash in the light; feet stamp on the ground; the flowers fly from the girls' hair; the sounds of voices and drums grow and grow, sobbing, thundering exultantly in one wild wave of sound. Then, suddenly, like native life itself, without climax, the drum stops, and the dancers are disappearing into the trees.

A French war-vessel bound for Eastern treaty ports arrived in the morning and anchored half a mile down the bay. Her officers, young and amusing, paid the *Cimba* a visit, remarked on her good hull, and considered her run from Nova Scotia to the Marquesas in sixty-odd days "most very pretty." Accepting an invitation to visit the warship, we set out in the collapsible tender, which, corked and braced, had come on degenerate days. I rowed, with Dombey, hunched in the stern, urging me on. The waves grew as we reached mid-harbour, and finally we shipped one green over the bow, foundered, came up, and, towing the tender, swam the rest of the way. It was the last service of the old tender before being converted into a fish-trap by the natives, and as the

Cimba was too small to house a rigid skiff, a canoe, or even a punt on deck it was never replaced.

The next visitor was the *La Korrigane*. We saw her white-bunted sails appear through the trees, and, going to the landing-place, greeted the ship's company on the beach. There was much to talk over, a great deal to be said all at once. The yacht had visited others of the Marquesas after sailing across the Pacific to tie with our time of nineteen days and establish a record—a great drive for a big vessel before indifferent weather. Running to our south, on one occasion she made 220 miles in a day. We offered to guide the new-comers about Tai-o-hae, but before long Mrs van den Broek disappeared with a drawing-pad, while the Countess, with more energy than any of us, finally grew impatient at our easy pace and hurried off in another direction. The company of the ladies lost, we broke up, I returning to the schooner, Dombey and the others setting off for the Resident's. The sun fell, it grew dark, and the land wind moaned until the *La Korrigane* and the *Cimba* were rolling side by side through another night.

The monthly trading schooner from Tahiti came in, un-loaded one or two cases of provisions, took aboard a few whale-boat loads of copra, and left. Then the *La Korrigane* got under way for a day at Taipi Bay before heading south-west 750 miles for Tahiti, where we spoke enthusiastically of meeting again. The next day, September 7, we took leave of the Marquesas, broke out sail, and ourselves headed for distant Tahiti.

When off soundings we saw the *La Korrigane* under the Nuka Hivan coast, her party evidently fishing. We held course in light airs until off the island of Ua Pu, a fantastic headland, a rough and shadowed sketch of pinnacles, minarets, towers, all of lava, exaggerated and lofted over the sea. The sun dropped, the wind fell, small stars came into the sky, and we hung motionless under the island. Some time in the night the *La Korrigane*, with diesels turning slowly, pressed through the calm unseen, overreached us, and took the lead.

In the morning, with the horizons empty, the *Cimba* sailed gently downhill, wing-and-wing, her sail shadows gliding, rising and falling on the swell. A red-fielded flag, showing her name in black, and known as the house flag, flew at the fore, together with the Bermudian *Victory*'s pennant. Exactly a year before the White 'Un had ceased to be a fisherman.

A seven-foot shark, which had followed us from Tai-o-hae, held to the counter. The sun grew hot, the sea resembled bluing water, and we decided to hold a sailor's holiday. After ripping up the floorboards to air the bilges we carried every scrap of clothing on deck, laid on the lifelines mattresses, old sail, and spare canvas, hoisted a string of clothes to the signal halyards, and stopped shirts, blankets, and dungarees to the stays with sail-twine. The schooner resembled an old-clothes shop rolling over the Pacific. Coming upon two respectable 'business suits,' last seen in Connecticut, now almost white with mildew, we decided that they would still bring a bunch or two of plantain. We stowed all this in the afternoon, tidied ship, and tried to discourage the shark under the counter, first with a steel shark hook, then, when this failed, by hitting him with a wingsail pole. But in the last of the day he was still there, following faithfully from a few yards astern.

In the next two days of light variables the schooner and shark covered 273 miles, which, for the former at least, was good work. The engine, its small tanks still full, was overhauled in readiness for Tahiti. The craft was touched up with paint; we cut each other's hair, set aside best shirts, and scrubbed clean our sand-shoes. Tactics were changed towards the shark, for, never having heard of one following a vessel, we became curious to see how long it would stay, enticing it with sea-biscuit as though it were a mascot. At night it proved company for the helmsman, falling astern when the *Cimba* lay out to a squall, gliding and nosing back when speed dropped.

Before making Tahiti from the north it is necessary to run through the Tuamotus, the Cloud Islands, a miraculous atoll chain spreading over sea between the 14th and 20th parallels of latitude and the 145th and 150th meridians. Southbound trading captains navigating Takaroa Passage, one of the channels of the group, where several islands must be passed close-on, try to pick up the first island before sunset, to ensure comparatively clear sailing until dawn, when, under normal conditions, the last should be sighted and the channel cleared. But we could not raise Takaroa, the most northern atoll, and passed on in the night without seeing it during the first watch. Consequently we were scarcely midway along the passage by morning. One after another Apataki, Aratiki, and Toau islands were brought to bear over the bows, hidden from view until almost run down, when suddenly above the lumpy trade-wind sea a cluster of furiously rolling palms would appear, cool, flashing, emerald. When very close on we had a glimpse of tree-trunks, a horizontal strip of sand, white and alive with shadow, narrow and only a foot or two above sea-level. At sunset there was left only Kaukura Island, a big atoll, well to the west; but as currents were both strong and uncertain course was set to clear the island by thirty miles. The moon came up, lit mare's-tails crisscrossing the sky, brightened the splashing sea, and showed the schooner logging five knots, gliding, stumbling.

The helmsman is alone in the steering-well, his legs stretched apart over the foot-brace, his arms close together sculling the tiller, his shirt open and drumming in the wind. He has been on some hours now, and steers not so much by the compass illuminated by moonlight as by feeling of the bite, the surge and the play of the craft herself. He is thinking; he is thinking of the good meals he is going to have in Tahiti, under the high mountains, beside those much talked-of lagoons. Perhaps some island chicken, a French salad, a tumbler of table-wine, a pot of black coffee. And then too, he meditates, the schooner will be in for a rest. She will be cleaned down, given moorings, and protected from the hurricane season, now only a few months off. How much will copper paint cost in Tahiti? And new halyards? Well, at any rate the old halyards can be rove off for sheets and preventers. And his mind returns to the subject of food. For almost a year now he has had an appetite, eaten three meals a day, often as many night lunches. It must be the salt air. And yet he has lost weight into the bargain. But then there are no weighty small-boat voyagers. It must be the eternal righting of oneself to keep with a little hull that does it, keeping one's balance throughout the watch. Then, too, a lack of exercise, cramped conditions, small-craft fare, and broken sleep must tell on the constitution. Perhaps these are more reasons why some trips break up at an early stage. Small-boating is not without its exactments. The helmsman looks over the area of ocean not hidden by the sails, and returns his gaze to the compass. Now at last, in these good latitudes, the sea—the blue drug of wind and space—can be trusted, at least for a few minutes at a time. He enlarges on this. "If," he says to himself, "I were to take a pair of dividers, place one point on the chart at the spot where we are now, and with the other draw a circle with a thousand-mile radius, I should perhaps be enclosing the finest sailing-grounds in the world." He glances up: something is blazing right by the bows, beyond the sails! A great wilderness of agitated silver shines close ahead, just a stone's-throw over the water. There is a roar, reverberating, rolling like thunder; and another. The *Cimba* is piling into a thousand thrashing palm-trees! The helmsman heaves the tiller over. There is no land: Kaukura's beach, heavy with ship-bones and almost underneath, is still invisible, and only a wall of windy trees, taller than the masts, are shown by the moon. He strains on the helm. The *Cimba* flings her head in a trough, staggers until the portholes suck water, spins on her heel, and drags out for sea-room. The sound of surf grows fainter and fainter in the distance.

After this incident of being carried by current thirty miles off-course in a few hours we squared away over open sea for Tahiti, losing our Marquesan shark, which for five days had cruised with us at the rate of more than a hundred miles a day.

FOURTEEN

TAHITI, PORT OF REFUGE

And there, on the Ideal Reef,
Thunders the Everlasting Sea.
            RUPERT BROOKE, *Tiare Tahiti*

FORTY-EIGHT hours later, two hundred miles farther on,
Dombey and I shared another landfall trick while the *Cimba*,
swinging silent cloths over ocean, nosed south-west without

breaking a bubble. We rode to her sway as though in the saddle, and for the first time since dropping the Marquesas held what might pass for a conversation, an aimless one, having Tahiti and its port Papeete (customarily pronounced to rhyme very nearly with Tahiti) for a subject. Could many of the written accounts, glowing and nostalgic, be relied upon? "Isle of Dreams," "fairy isles," "isles of enchantment. . . ." The schooner lurched to port; the deck-horses rang sharply. Then she settled down. On the other hand, there was J. B. Priestley's *Faraway*, telling of an island without a virtue, besides the accounts of those who, equipped with a photographer, can step off a passenger boat and find the evil heart of any given place in almost any given time. Perhaps, after all, the island of which so much has been written was just another dot on a Pacific chart, overrated, dissolute, brought upon bitter days.

The helmsman kept sharp look-out. The constellations wested, the false dawn came and went, and the wind dropped. At daybreak a mountain was sighted on the rim-line, the trades came to life, and we quickened pace. Near noon Tahiti lifted high above the noisy indigo sea sweeping by our white paint, a tilting wave of land, blue with valleys, green with tall, ascending ridges. Following a sweep of coast-line, gaudy in downpouring sunlight, we ran for the port, Papeete. For once the trades held, increased, until we scud-ded before the stinging warmth with bows lifting, stern set-tling, and buff-painted booms stabbing the whirling sea.

Farther inshore ran lanes of darker water; the wind sucked harder, and we fancied that the *Cimba* was almost tipping ten knots off Point Venus and Matavai Bay, the old anchoring-place, choppy in sunshine.

What a day to come in from the sea! Oh, my heart, what a day! Holding to the curves of lagoons, the schooner ran wing-and-wing, racing by the reefs, her canvas bunted against the shrouds, her flags whipped and tossed, going mad overhead. The sea bombarded the near-by coral, and sent spray twisting down-wind, catapulting it on to sunny lagoons—here and there a canoe in slow drift, and beyond a sweep of beach, wide-curved under palms waving over a hut, a tropical house; then, steep-to, the mountains climbing so many shadows to meet an in-sweeping tide of cloud, blazing, streaked with columns of moving, vertical light. To starboard the ocean tumbled, flinging itself out to the wind. Moorea, the sister island, lay upon it, a cold block of blue, heavy on its brim. Unerringly the *Cimba* slashed home, her bows clean-cutting the driving sea, tripped past an inward-bound trading schooner of rusted chain-plates, and ran down a bonito launch, steaming under a squadron of screaming birds. Far ahead, off Papeete Reach, the sails of another schooner showed for a moment, then disappeared beyond the pass. A pair of wireless masts came into view, a low group of buildings, the tower of a church, the white mast of a signal station.

Two cable-lengths to windward of the pass a large cross-sea sucked into the entrance, drove aboard, and buried the rail. The bows swerved a quarter-circle, and the foresail jibbed with a loud report, hung loose, and flapped wildly. We threw the halyards off the pins, bringing the sail down on the run, to find the gaff parted at the jaws—our first accident in the Pacific. Carried by four long swells, the *Cimba*, the smallest craft to gain Tahiti, came into harbour seven days a few hours from the Marquesas, having logged nine and a half knots, as clocked ashore, from off Point Venus.

The quarantine ground indicated on the chart lay at the edge of a comfortable harbour and almost a mile from the port proper. Fetching it, we anchored in the chop, dropped sail, hoisted the yellow 'Q' signal, and stood by for the authorities. The blazing decks rolled; we perspired and breathed deeply of a wind drenched with the odour of flowers, an odour overwhelming, unique, which must for ever distinguish Tahiti from a thousand other islands. We waited, coiling down the gear, harbour-furling the sails. The sea, coloured and sunny, began breaking; the hook started to drag.

"Just like these people!" we commented somewhat unpleasantly. "Know we're foreigners . . . hold us to a bad anchorage . . . want to see us drag and pile up on the reef" —outbursts that often occur at the end of a 'dream voyage'; the accumulation of minor strains that must never be revealed while under way, now flooding to the surface when the sails are furled, when progress has ceased and the very purpose of life seems to disappear with the drowning of the anchors; when that delicate instrument a sailing craft, which for so long now has registered every rhythm of elements stretching to every shore, is suddenly brought to a stop, to jerk at her chains, to pound indelicately, rolling like a drunken sailor off the new-found port; and invariably, for a moment at least, the crew is overtaken by a feeling of nausea, by a desire to scud to sea—for another submergence, another helping of that windy blue drug.

They did not come! The anchor, which had slowly broken ground, suddenly tripped, and the schooner made sternway towards a strip of shoal. Dombey ran to the storeroom and set the motor in action, while I fished anchor. We pitched to windward, cutting the slop, making a great deal of noise. Presently the engine, silent for so long, was shocking our senses, hurting unaccustomed ears. The carefully furled sails were set again, the motor stopped, and we stood off-and-on over the quarantine grounds. A sailing canoe flashed by; a figure leaned over a tilted outrigger, waving a straw hat as he drove for the land.

A launch, flying the tricolour, came alongside, and there jumped aboard a rather slender man in whites, who shook us by the hand. "We've been expecting you," he said with a grin, "but you are so small, so *petite*, the smallest we've welcomed. Why, from on shore you are just a little canoe!" The doctor joined the port captain. "Welcome, messieurs!"

He glanced at the bill of health, ordered us to lower the quarantine signal, then with a bow returned to the pilot boat. We started to hoist the rapidly lowered canvas for the last time. "No, no," said the Captain; "we'll give you a tow." A line was passed to the launch, we began to move, and the Captain, smiling benevolently, reached for the tiller. All port captains love to steer.

Before long we were aware of a new sound, the echo of a chant having neither more nor less meaning than the wind; the surging of a town, as restless as a breaking reef, a dull discordancy unfamiliar since Panama. The land seemed to reach out, to gauntlet the schooner, to strip her of her freedom, of her illusions as well as her sails, of her slight but immaculate power. Slow and measured chimes struck in the belfry of an invisible limestone cathedral. "Let go your towline! Let go! . . ." We drifted to berth beside a curved retaining wall covered by trees half burying the single line of business houses; drifted into a fleet of white schooners lying stern-to off the greensward of the Quai du Commerce. We heard a cheer over-water, and, looking up, saw the bowsprit of our mooring mate manned by seamen waving berets, by men of Bordeaux. The *La Korrigane* was at anchors! It was she whom we had seen entering the passage half an hour before. We waved, secured the *Cimba* under the trees, and made for the shore.

The slight case of nerves and melancholy was over with, and underfoot the earth, plastic yet rigid, and to be covered only by effort, had a pleasant, almost sensuous feel. We rolled as little as possible, turned from the shore, and climbed *La Korrigane's* gangway. Charlie van den Broek greeted us from the taffrail. "My dear fellows! How good! How good! . . ." The others stood smiling behind him.

We were walking over the brown earth of the Quai du Commerce, Papeete's main road, under trees that heaved cool, windy shadows upon the road, upon the low-roofed, grass-fronted business houses, and upon the backs, the breasts, the faces, of the passers-by—Tahitian men, open-shirted, in tall pandanus hats, Europeans in exactly the same dress; Europeans in whites, in khaki, in stiff nineteenth-century tunics, in pipe-clay boots and pith helmets, in old dungarees; Tahitian girls, delicately featured, thin, heavy, square-headed, round-headed, with Christian-like smiles and heathen laughter—the stiff-nostrilled glare of the goddess, the white and parted teeth of the temptress, the wistful eyes of the unloved; old flower-sellers, bony, drooped as though in a trance over the beauty they had picked; the head, the heaving shoulders, of a schooner captain, a dotted silk kerchief clapped about a faded straw hat; a priest, the trail of his black gown touching the road, wearing a white cork helmet, a dark beard; a Chinaman or two beside unmoving barrows—a hundred luxuries and beloved trinkets stowed in little glass boxes—spare and child-like of form, with the dreamy eyes of those lost in the profound possibilities of commerce.

We pause beneath a white veranda facing the sea. The kaleidoscope is behind, and we look over our shoulders at the crowd. But there is no crowd at all! To be sure, the black-frocked priest is still moving under the shade, the skipper has stopped to lean against a tree to gaze sternly, intimately, at his command beyond the wharf, and the flower-sellers lie lifeless as ever on the pathway. Here and there a figure in sunshine, in shade, the glitter of a bicycle, the phantom of a motor-car; perhaps thirty souls are passing the quay—no more. A blast of trade wind rolls against the trees, shuffling the deceiving shadows, while beneath the heavy leaves rays of reflected sea-shine glow on old brick, grow dim, and flare again. The shipping rocks at anchor, and a fine spray blows over the grass . . . "Bon jour, messieurs! . . ." Stiff of leg, we ascend to the veranda, welcomed by Mr Alex Sturgois, and there, with our French friends, toast one another's craft: "To the white ladies. God bless 'em!"

A stout meal: limed papaya, Vienna schnitzel and rice, blocks of gravied carrot, French bread, tinned New Zealand butter, native beer, cake, and Chinese ice-cream, with black scented coffee. And mail: letters from the Steel Age, tender and fearsome and heroic.

When we left for the *Cimba* the wind had dropped, and the trees moved no more over the trading-places locked for the night. Above the calm harbour a sky of pearl shell was losing colour. The Chinamen with barrows were lighting their lanterns in the still air. A squall of laughter came from the deck of a trader, whose crew, gathered at supper, were soon to sail for the Austral Islands. The schooners lay quiet along the

curving wall: the *Potii Raiatea*, with a cargo from Les Iles sous
le Vent, the *Denise*, home from the Marquesas, the perfect
little *Vaite*, *Tiare Tepora*, the *Romona*, *Gisbourne*, the able
Manireva, a country craft, the *Moano*, largest of the white,
bright-sparred fleet—each equipped with a whole foresail, a
steadying mainsail, and all save one moderately dieseled. A
few cutters floated beside them, traders also, warped to the
silent quay, to the hub of trade, as it were, of a cartwheel of islands beyond. And, as with the fishermen of Nova Scotia, the
profits of the fleet did not justify its scrupulous upkeep. But
so often is it the case where there are sails. Owners, skippers,
paid hands, look to them with homely last-century senti-
ments, with a bluff regard that has nothing at all to do with
mere money-making; to the sails that have kept them out in
the night, brought them to fear, tested their courage, their
faith. And given them? Well, something more, and yet bit-
terly less, than their most profitable cargo.

The fleet awaited the monthly steamer. She came in of a
morning, green-painted, with a smokestack of scarlet, took on
some bags of copra, deposited mail, fifteen passengers, and a
few cargo-slings of goods, and departed. Shortly after she left
the *Cimba* was taken for a haul-out, and *La Korrigane* sailed to
spend the hurricane season off New Zealand fishing-grounds.
The two-hundred-tonner and the five-tonner, after five thousand miles of smart sailing that had carried them to port half
an hour apart—a worthy feat for the smaller, a greater one,
in view of the light winds, for the larger—were parting at last.

It was arranged that Singapore should be the next rendezvous—"if," we would add provisionally. "But there are no 'ifs,'" Count de Ganay would reply. "Why, you'll beat us this time—by an hour at least. . . ." She ran the pass cleanly, her good, wholesome model pitching until the large topsail was sheeted home, to steady her solid spars. A gallant sight, she disappeared to the westward.

Shored up on the beach, the *Cimba* was wire-scrubbed below the water-line, and thoroughly inspected. Well-liked from the very first by the natives, who have ever an eye for a boat, she came to be admired by the whites as well, one resident commissioning Thomas Ellacott, a very capable local shipwright, to copy her lines with a view to building a sister craft. When she had been painted and floated we moored her in a lagoon twelve kilometres from town, to lie in refuge until the close of the hurricane season. This done, Dombey and I separated until the time came to go on. Although we often said that only in port did we come to know each other, we needed a holiday to release us from the intimacy imposed by the cruise. Men or boys are seldom emotionally balanced to stand the strain of sharing interminable solitude. Hermits do not wander in pairs, and it is one thing to spend a week in close company with a friend; quite another, a month, a year. Emotions, temperaments, psychological balances, often break cruises at an early stage. They are the forces behind the scene, forces that above all others must be mastered in voyaging.

Dombey tossed a coin. I laughed at his bad luck, and, hurriedly filling an old grip, made for the shore, to search for a home on Tahiti. I did not look long before settling in a semi-native hut of bamboo and pandanus, facing a lagoon at the edge of an estate known as the Governor Morris Place, then occupied by my good friend Robert Minturn. Before long Dombey had made at least partial quarters ashore, at the house of Fara, a native, who, together with his wife and children, no less than worshipped him. The hurricane season arrived. But Tahiti, to the east and south of the cyclonic track, is a favoured island, rarely touched by more than the tail of a storm, and the *Cimba* floated safely in the lagoon through long days of calm and nights of aimless drift, on one side protected by the mountains, on the other by a barrier reef.

Tahiti is a round island, possibly thirty miles across, with a bulging peninsula, known as Tairarapou—little Tahiti— on its south-eastern coast. The mountains, claiming almost the entire island, are uninhabitable, and the fourteen thousand inhabitants live under the hills on a profusely vegetated base circling the island at sea-level. An eighty-mile road rounds the coast, heavy with fruit, wild with flowers, and covered by the eternal coconut palms, filtering the harsh, unmodulated sunlight. And there upon this foreshore, between mountains and sea, are the homes of the people.

And the natives themselves? Sophisticated? Fallen? Dissolute? There are hints of all this, but there is also a great deal more—the charm, the graciousness, romanticists had seen, the warm hearts, the sincerity, and the nobility of an unacquisitive, uncalculating race.

Memories of Tahiti: the unending odour of flowers moving like tides of scent, of salt winds blowing through mango and plots of lime-trees. Moorean sunsets, with purple canoes and purple figures in slow movement before the overcoloured west that leaves them so quickly in darkness; a second of moonlight catching the eyes, the warm flowers of singing islanders; and female forms, shiny, firm, bent over a river of dusk. The reef-line at night glowing with the torches of fishermen moving in wavering pilgrimage towards the sea; clear-cut green mornings and shaded, comfortable days of rain; sunlight flashing on to a lagoon, on to yellow huts and red dresses, on to the varnished green of palm-fronds. And the underwater of lagoons—bubbles breaking from the nose, the body pressed in by bottle-green salt, a fish spear wavering before the eyes. Sounds: the rumble of a Chinaman's cart *en route* through a forest of palm; the song of a girl, of a guitar with a broken string or two; the slash of palms, the surge of the lagoon, the breaking of ocean water, rumbling reef, the slow suck of backwash; the tense, melodramatic whine of a vicious, hard-flung squall, high-pitched and coursing over ocean wet and windy for the trembling headland.

October, and lighter winds from the eastward as the trades die out. November, and a sun of southern declination;

the oranges ripening in the valley. December, and heat without unusual humidity, the rains generously punctuated by fair weather, the breadfruit becoming edible. January and February, and calms, with sudden winds rounding the compass. March, and the fear of hurricanes to the west and north diminishing; the return of the trades blowing gently home out of the south-east.

Quite suddenly it became time to set out for the Leeward Group, where the reach towards the Samoas would begin. The schooner was beached, painted, set back in the sea, and moored off the Papeete waterfront for fitting out. All manner of equipment had been earned for her by donning swashbuckling wigs and swinging property cutlasses before the frantic movie cameras of a company deposited by the mail-boat to make a costly South Seas romance. And now her new hand, George M. Taggart, an American, joined, as Dombey, for reasons not then to be pried from him, was to leave at Pago Pago, Samoa. Taggart resembled Dombey and me in that he was of fair height. Narrow-hipped, broad of shoulder, he had a nautical inclination towards slimness. He wore a moustache, spoke five languages, and was a good spinner of yarns. During his thirty-three years he had been, in turn, lumberjack, trader in Siberia, sailor, plantation overseer in South-western Mexico, pearl-diver in Oceania, prospector of the Yukon and the Arctic Circle. When won over by the trip, or, to be more exact, by the schooner, it was on just returning to Tahiti, via Turkistan and Persia,

Australia, New Zealand, and Raratonga, from an expedition into Afghanistan and Tibet.

All day there had been bustle, but at last the multiple tasks of clearing at the harbour master's office, checking provisions, taking on water, putting the engine in trim, sweating up lanyards, lifelines, and sail-lacing, were finished. These over, Dombey and Taggart had disappeared for the suddenly darkened shore, confident that we should get away at sunrise. I paused on deck with a bitter unlighted pipe. Crouched on the retaining wall, a yard beyond the stern, an old woman, thin, almost blind, was weaving a tall crowned hat under a flaring lamp. Chinamen stood vigil beside dim lanterns, and in the darkness an upstairs veranda of a club glowed like a suspended stage. That would be my good friend Arthur Brander, a gentleman of the Old World, at the head of a table occupied by a few lounging figures in whites. I glanced once more at the native woman. Her fingers moved as surely as they had at breakfast-time. She was from distant Mangireva Island, and it was rumoured that she had been weaving ever since 1917, when, refusing to believe her son killed in France, she set out to find him. Tahiti, of course, would be the most difficult to reach, but once there "'Frisco" (where the mailboat goes) could not be far away, and no distance at all from her lost son. Saving the occasional francs earned by weaving, she had after eighteen years enough to take passage on the trading schooner that only a day ago had landed her at Papeete. Her fingers stopped moving as the *Cimba*'s warps creaked to the low wind. She lifted her head; some saucy Tahitian girls were taunting a Chinaman. With loud laughter they abandoned their small prey even as she watched, and headed up-street, languorous, heavily scented, on the look-out, not for riches or miracles, but only for more of laughter, for life—lusting for it! And they were right, and the barrow-pushing Chinaman with only a conventional lust for money was hopelessly wrong, as his face, peeking over his lantern, quite clearly showed. Two half-castes, lovers, high of head, stopped a moment before his barrow, took large slices of watermelon, flung down some coins, and swayed proudly on. Faint sounds of music rang, thumped in the air. Suddenly the lights of the club went out: "Good night . . . *Bon soir . . . Au revoir. . . .*" And the road had given itself over to darkness and the low hum of wind. I looked at the old woman. Protected by a dress of black, she lay outstretched on the stone, one arm about the weaving-block, the other shielding her face, fast asleep.

Early on the morning of May 5, 1935, we got under way for the island of Raiatea, the Green Cloud. A few friends stood on the wharf, their backs to the shuttered business block, closed for Sunday. I looked at Tahiti for the last time, looked closely into her pensive eyes, at the wistfulness of her parted lips courageous with forced laughter, at her winded hair wild with sunshine, at the curve of a waving hand. Tahiti, brave with love, *is* enchanted. All loved things are.

How well would the three-man crew work? A trio, perhaps unique, if only that each member had served time aboard commercial square-riggers, might operate very well. They might! We ran down-harbour in a fresh breeze, then tacked for channel. At the end of the second tack it appeared that by passing a marker close on we should get clear. Being at the tiller, I called out and asked if the chart showed deep water immediately outside of the marker. A voice answered, "Yes," and we pitched for some yards into the sun-flash. Suddenly there was a crashing sound forward, and the craft became rigid, immovable. I leaped over the rail, gained a barefooted purchase on the reef, put my shoulders against the bilge, and heaved as hard as I could. A sea lifted the hull, the keel grated, cleared, and I had to swing aboard quickly to keep with it. Before we could change tack we stumbled again, with wood on coral. Taggart joined me in the sea, and together we hove her clear. But she hit again, this time solidly, with the wind canting the deck steeply, pressing the lee rail to water-level. Fifty yards off a roller was bearing down. Not only must we get clear, but on to the other tack as well. Foresail and jib sheets were let on the fly. A wingsail pole was slashed adrift, and Dombey, jumping into a sea now above our waists, worked with me, applying the pole as a lever between bow and reef. We strained the spar to breaking-point, while Taggart, entirely under water, threw his weight against the stern-post. The bow moved, came up in the wind, and idled off to the other side. The pole was flung aboard. One of us climbed on, took in the sheets, then dived back to help the others move the last of the keel off the shoal. We moved it, the roller hit, and broke, but we were clear, and instead of throwing us back the swell lifted the craft, which, taking a capful of wind, began to sail as we swarmed aboard.

The trio, quite subdued, bent over gashed feet and legs. The three-man crew had come to grief in the first few minutes in an obvious, lubberly manner. There had been confusion and noise aboard. The question regarding the marker had not been answered, the chart not looked at, and the affirmative answer I heard was directed not at me, but at the third man. Each one of us had depended upon the other two, and we had run without caution. Never mind! It wouldn't happen again: we were so sure as we set about bathing our cuts.

The wind died, the sails rocked against the sunset, and at dusk Tahiti disappeared, a tolerant body of land with an aura of dusky peace feeling out over the ever-demanding sea. The *Cimba* just moved, and no more. There was a supper of rice, fried fish, tea. Before midnight rain fell, and a wind arose. When Taggart, wet through, came below at twelve I thought to ask how he had found the first trick.

"Well," he replied, with a fierce pull at his moustache, "I don't know what it is, but something about it vaguely reminds me of yachting."

Dombey's voice: "Close that hatchway! Here's a squall clamping down!"

FIFTEEN

AN OCEAN RACE—THE ISLANDS UNDER THE WIND

MORNING, with no land in sight, with the sea silent under grey cloud and given over to what old-time crews would have called a 'clock' calm or a Paddy's hurricane—an 'up-and-down wind' that had disappeared 'walking Spanish.' Although clouds were lighted by 'devil's smiles' of sunlight piercing their wetness, the weather became dense, visibility was lost, a confused sea started to throw up, and before long a rainy 'nose-ender' was wailing over the bows. Strange South Seas weather! The rigging tautened, the dead-work buried under to the wash-boards, and with sails flat, bows a-pitch and flushing, the *Cimba* dived into a hollow, curling sea. Suddenly, unexpectedly, land appeared close on through the muck: an instant of confusion, the helm thrown down, the clash of sheet harness yanking at the travellers as the bows, arcing into the rain, staggered a moment, then slouched for sea-room on a new tack.

There had been another blunder! There should be clear sailing until late afternoon; furthermore, the land sighted was not Raiatea at all, but Huahine, another Lee Island. In less than a hundred miles' work the three-man crew, without the aid of current, had been set more than thirty miles off course! Gruff words passed in the demoralized pause that followed. Restraint was cast aside. But this would never do, and we rallied for self-control, for a certain indispensable sanity, until the error was calmly brought to light. After swinging ship in Papeete for compass deviation the engine had been taken down, then set back to acquire new magnetic centres, affecting the compass. And, this done, we had failed to swing ship again. But we should learn now, we should do far better in the future, and each of us, prompted by some blind force to keep his personality at arm's-length from the other personalities, would drown the impulse, an Anglo-Saxon vanity, or whatever it was, and become a whole-hearted slave to that godhead the craft. So in a moment capable of breaking up the cruise we came together, a unit for the first time.

To avoid sailing blind with unknown compass error we went back on the old tack, heeled cautiously for land, and jigsawed along coast until sighting the pass to the village. With scuppers under and the red farewell ribbon received in Tahiti flagging taut at the jib-stay, we ran the pass and gained the lagoon, to throw anchors off a beach grey in the rain and lined by doll-like huts, fragile beneath heavy water-colour clouds.

Finally the rain stopped, the wind fell, the island became lighted, green, and the sea brilliantly glassy. We dived overside to take toll of the damage suffered off Papeete, finding only a few scratches on the hull and the iron of the keel bare of paint. Going ashore, we inspected the village of Fare, made friends with the people, and after a native supper brought from on board a gramophone, the lately received and most welcome gift of Mr and Mrs Tucker McClure, the friends of our Canal Zone days. In the concert that followed at the chief's place we forgave a lack of appreciation for Bach and Brahms, the indifference with which jazz was received, and spent a late evening playing over and over again three lovely Hawaiian records. Finally, when even the good-natured chief had had enough, we sauntered to the beach to be paddled home by a young native singing a Hawaiian melody with improvised Tahitian words. At nine in the morning, with the compass checked by shore bearings, we lifted sail for Raiatea, standing off before the push of light winds from the south.

Raiatea's sacred peak, Temehani, stands over the principal village of Uturoa, situated on a spare stretch of shore. Beyond is a plane of protected water reaching for the island of Tahaa, a wide strait alive with sailing canoes keeling to the south-east trade. These craft are of sharp models, built of strakes of redwood sewn together with coir rope, and set sprit-sails of moderate head, the sprit being vanged to a length of bumpkin shipped over the stern. On one tack the outrigger to leeward buoys them; on the other, when weighted by the crew, it serves as outside ballast. Off-wind the canoes come near to being slow-coaches, but with sheets in, the sea calm, and the breeze strong their turn of speed is nothing short of amazing.

On going ashore we found Uturoa a ghost of the pre-depression days of the Tin Roof Era. Cottages and huts, their metal topping occasionally red with protective paint, but more often with rust, lay along the well-built but little-used roads that wander from the remaining store-houses, the long-abandoned cinema, a silent inn. Fortunes in copra had come and gone—as strange dreams, first visualized, then lost, leaving the Chinamen to mourn their disappearance and the white traders to talk of the old days, to sigh; to begin all over again; only the natives, as though armed with the philosophy of gods, had fully forgotten.

When Dombey and Taggart went off together I wandered about the village, limping somewhat from the cuts on my feet. I met a French planter, who, having followed the *Cimba's* story in the *Rudder*, had long hoped that she would show up at Raiatea. At the inn an old man, sipping wine and smoking an American cigarette, informed me with Pickwickian flavour that *he* had set out for the South Seas at seventy-five. That would be five years ago, for on this very day he had turned eighty. No, he'd never go back. No longer was there glory in growing old at home. They looked upon you as an invalid, kept you out of things—killed you! Down here he would forever be treated as a gentleman, as a man. No, he'd rest his old bones right here, thank you. And he gave me a sly wink, the wink of some one who feels that he's cheated the established order of things and got away with it.

In the morning the trading schooner arrived, surrounded by canoes and cutters, their crews clamouring more for Tahitian news than for goods. "Cargo and gossip is my main freights," the skipper would say, laughing. All that day she lay beside the wharf, the centre of activity, of bustle, of laughter. She left at sunset, disappearing together with the low sails of canoes, staggering out of sight before a hard south-easter. And that evening we acquired a passenger, a native of Bora Bora, our next island, who was desperate to reach the bedside of his sick child.

We sailed at daybreak towards the tall peak of Bora Bora, thirty miles away, passing over the shallows of Peupea Channel, a barely submerged valley once connecting Raiatea and Tahaa. Some five hundred yards from shore the *Cimba* was overtaken by a native riding horseback off her beam. The hocks of the galloping horse just cleared the water, and the rider closed in until a sudden depression of the channel caused him to stop a few yards away. He caught the red packet of 'Tinto' tobacco thrown him, shouted gaily, waved, and turned his charge, the horse setting off in one direction, the schooner in another.

Leaving the channel astern, we carried along a great barrier reef, found a pass, jammed into it, threw one sheaf of spray to the mast-tops, and gained open ocean. "*Goot potii!*" laughed Faraa, the native, forgetting to grieve for his child. The wind blew, the sun shone, and before long the schooner was racing past a ring of bright outlying islands surrounding the magnificent Temanu, that overwhelming spire of mountain canted over the Bora Boran shore. Before long she was tied up off the village of Vaitope, and Faraa was on the beach asking for news of his child. He came back frightened. The boy, lying on the other side of the island, had not slept in nine days! What could be done? Dombey and Taggart--my feet would not stand a long hike—prepared to find out. The two medicine kits were ransacked, as was the tool-rack over the engine. An assortment of pills was spilled from one of the kits, and before a word could be said Faraa scooped the lot from the deck, swallowing every one, as he explained, to ease his grief.

They returned the following day, announcing a complete cure. I believe it was Dombey who administered a large dose of castor-oil, Taggart who removed a tooth with engine-room pliers. At any rate, they were very pleased with themselves, and spared no pains in describing the joy of the parents, the disparagement of the local medicine-man, and the feasts following their success. Borrowing a canoe, we made a rough lugsail of native cloth and set out over Te-ava-nui Water for Motu Muté, Motu Omé, Teviroa, and Tupua —the islets that surround the fantastically beautiful Bora Bora. On Tupua, after a long search, an ancient sacrificial altar was found, and near by a pinnacle of lava giving forth a bell-like sound when struck, which in olden days was used to summon the natives to the altar. We returned, not soon to forget those out islands—their caves of palm, whirlwinds of shadows, dark mystery; the white beaches without a footprint, running beside a splashing sea, windy, warm-coloured throughout the day, calm and scarlet as we sailed home in the sunset.

Returning to Vaitope, we found a yacht, the *Potii Farani*, the only craft of the lonely island of Maupiti, riding at anchors. A good six feet longer than the *Cimba*, she was of an able model, sweet of line, amply masted—all in all a worthy rival for the Bluenoser. And this she was to be, as we, also bound for Maupiti, accepted a challenge from her crew.

At 7 A.M. on May 17 both craft got under way, the *Potii Farani* with a native crew of six and one Gerlac, a young

German wanderer whom we had first seen in Tahiti, then in Raiatea, and the *Cimba* with eight passengers aboard— Tira, an ancient Maupitian, stranded on Bora Bora for more than a year; Tu, a large, happy native, who could never save a franc for the fare home; his wife, Clotira, their grown daughter, and four little girls, all of whom had been marooned from Maupiti for over three years. When the sails were set the womenfolk, refusing to go below, prepared for sea in the manner of all Polynesian women, binding cloths tightly about their middles before lying on deck, prostrate, covered head to foot in white sheets, neither to stir nor speak until Maupiti was gained.

Side by side schooner and yawl ran for Te-ava-nui Pass, neither one able to lead the other to sea. Reaching open ocean, they drew fair, light winds, in which the handsome yawl pulled away, heading for Maupiti, thirty miles due west. With Gerlac, the German, playing a harmonica on her deck, she crept out ahead, lifting neatly to a sea just making up, until finally Tu, standing on our deck ridiculing the other crew, grew comparatively quiet, and old Tira, with a lure of pearl-shell wagered on the schooner, subsided into philosophical silence.

Running wing and wing, we attempted to pull under the yawl's stern, blanketing her sails with our smaller ones. We failed. When a wingsail was set to aid the foresail and mainsail the crew of the yawl broke out a big spinnaker, ran a smaller one up the jigger, and to catch draughts between main and spinnaker hoisted a fifth sail, a catch-all jib, filling over the bowsprit. At that point, however, a series of gusts favoured our quarter; the *Cimba* hurried, closed the lead, ran under the yawl's counter, came alongside, carried way, and took a full length lead—amid loud shouting, led by Tu, who, leaning overside, hurled insult upon insult at the men of Maupiti. As the deck began to cant we secured lanyards about the immovable women, only one of whom stirred, and then only to give Tu an inscrutable look. The lead was held, the shouting turned to laughter, and as we swayed over the sea the natives of both craft began to sing, while Gerlac, the wanderer, struck up an Island song.

Ten minutes passed, the variables withdrew before the steadier, lighter trade wind, and the yacht-like *Potii Farani* drew abeam, and despite the jeers of our vociferous passenger swept ahead. The heretofore unbeaten Bluenoser, her bow spooning water, fell farther and farther astern, to taste defeat, which, like despair, like hope, like victory itself, must, in the blind acceptance of all revelations, also be known first-hand. And now one thing became certain: the trade wind would grow no bolder. It had set in for the day, a wide wind not to fluke, increase, or diminish, to favour neither craft over the remaining twenty-odd miles. Old Tira steered, Tu amused himself with a harpoon; we held the after-deck, meditating in the sun, while gently the sea rocked the freight of shrouded women.

An hour and a half went by, and then, with Maupiti rising

quickly in the west, and the yawl running in miniature quarter of a mile out in front, Dombey suggested that we were holding our own. All hands watched, gauging the separating space. Finally there could be no doubt but that the *Cimba* had begun to hang on, and at the end of another fifteen minutes' work we knew that she had taken in a little of the lead. Rolling her fisherman's shear, setting astern a noisy flow of white drift, working with her cut-water, she began to march out to her rival with the half-drunk, half-graceful movements of a scudding craft. We could make nothing of it, nothing at all. The wind, favouring neither vessel, had not altered direction or velocity. The yawl appeared to be moving as unconcernedly as ever, to be aided by every ounce of her canvas as the *Cimba* closed in, a slug of broken water under her foot; and we knew that as crews we were not outsailing the Maupitians, who were managing their craft as adroitly as ever our schooner was being handled.

The two craft came together, lunging over a skeleton-work of spume, diving, swinging in the trade-wind chop, rolling their cloth over vast, shadowless space, tense with movement, restrained, dancing rather than racing, leaving their crews to the calculation of results.

With old Tira at the helm, we moved out in front and reached for the black hills of Maupiti, rising into the sky. Now the turn-about was explained. It had been calm at the outset, but the trades, returning after a night of rest, had not been long in forcing up a short, steep sea, causing the yawl to labour more and more, the schooner to begin planing on rough capped water. Hull-lines, not sail-power, had brought about the unexpected. The *Potii Farani*, for all her good looks, had a bow that was inclined to be walled, a type found occasionally in yachts insufficiently 'appled' to run down-sea; a bow designed primarily for slicing to windward, not for all-round work, and certainly not for bolstering a sail-press before sharpened wave formations. And she had one last defect. As in many yawls and ketches, the mainmast was stepped, without rake, so far forward that while running the bows became overburdened and staggered, rolling the wind out of the sails.

As the *Cimba* went by the natives of the yawl cheered, answered Tu's catcalls, and appeared quite pleased that the schooner was to show them home. For there was no catching her. The breaking sea pleased her, she planed crest to crest, forged through the troughs, and drew up off Maupiti Pass half a mile ahead of the yawl.

The race was over, and now something of a more serious nature lay ahead, that of shooting the pass, a dangerous inlet holding the island of Maupiti and its immense lagoon in eternal isolation. Even while laying-to quarter of a mile in the offing we could see a great play of water rushing the coral barrier, and hear the boom of heavy surf above the wind. The yawl drew up, the lower edges of her sails wet with spray, her crew shouting for us to precede them—etiquette of the Islands, no doubt. Rolling wildly, they brought up into the eye of the wind and stopped to watch us enter. We did not hurry. The women and girls were untied, and after much persuasion, aided by the energetic and jubilant Tu, were sent below. The wingsail was carefully stowed, the boom unshipped and secured between the shrouds, the mainsail and jib were brought down, the foresail was close-sheeted to act as a steadying sail, and the engine, primed for the occasion, was set going, to be vigilantly tended by Dombey. The noisy Tu was brought to silence. With decks cleared and the motor running smoothly we headed for the passage. I kept forward to con from the bow, Taggart stationed himself beside Tira, our pilot, whose eyesight we had yet to learn was failing, while Tu, his lips pressed tightly together, crouched in the waterways.

Twenty yards off the entrance a languid swell moved in, glided for the stern, elevated us, paused. The inclining top of glass moved slowly, curved, mounted, acquired an edge, a thin line of agitated water that arose, trembled, grew higher, whiter, broke, exploded, and flung us headlong at a narrow coral mouth. Down into a mill-stream, green and foaming, barred with eddies and wild currents, we ran, at ten—eleven knots. The bows swerved, uncontrolled; the engine coughed, missed a stroke, continued. A woman screamed; then the noise of the pass drowned out all sound. A triangular wave caught us, half submerged us, ricocheted us into the coral to starboard; the helm was jammed over, the masts jumped, the entire rigging quivered. The bow cut past the coral, missing it by yards, angled down-water, headed for mid-channel, into an island of bright submerged coral, then, forced over by propeller, by rudder, drew away just in time, curving in a quick arc into the slash of a whirlpool. The hull trembled. A mass of water lifted over the bows, hiding the island ahead. Some one shouted, "She's through!" The water fell away and we were shooting between two walls of palm-trees, running downhill into a large and placid lagoon.

With a sigh I turned aft. Tu was still in a crouching position, but the runaway schooner had been too much for the amiable Tira, and I saw that Taggart, a smile on his face, had taken the helm in a crucial moment. Over their heads the flying *Potii Farani* was running the pass, with coral close aboard to either side, her bows in foam, her masts lurching wildly. In another moment she had swept through, to join us off the two islands at the edge of the lagoon. Some one laughed, flung open the companion, and ordered the women on deck. Dombey appeared from the after-hatch—the hero of the occasion, having struggled successfully to bring the failing engine back to action within the dark and rolling storeroom. Every one was happy. Tu, himself once more, kissed the women and children, who turned on reaching deck, looked at their home island, and cried!

The two vessels left the uninhabited islets astern, crossed the lagoon where a wide spit of sand stretched far to the eastward, and tied up at the landing-place beneath the cliffs of Maupiti, a melancholy confusion of stone, stained, black, and resembling the ruins of a gigantic castle—exactly as promised by the poetic description in the Hydrographic Sailing Directions. Never before had two vessels reached

Maupiti together, and the people, perhaps three hundred in all, swarmed excitedly about the craft. Tu, brimming over, exuberant, threw his arms about old friends, kissed the women, while Tira, in his best Paumotuian, tried to explain a year's absence to an ancient wife, who, though apparently deaf, was certainly by no means mute. There was much laughter, some weeping. The crew of the yawl cheered the *Cimba*; the crew of the *Cimba* cheered the yawl. Then the *Potii Farani's* master, praising the schooner, came up with his son Farno, the mate. We must live with them—we must! Then Tu declared that we must stay with him, arguing vehemently until the crowd roared with laughter. They knew that the light-hearted Tu had no house at all, that he and his wife and children must all live together in his mother's one-roomed hut. So, after schooner and yawl were anchored in the lagoon, and after many protests, we set off with Piau Terope and Farno to spend some of the pleasantest days in the islands at their little grass house, its caged veranda of split bamboo directly under cliffs threatening the muddy land, the humble village.

It has been often said that bountiful lagoons and amply wooded and vegetated shores account for all the generous qualities of the Polynesians, intimating that goodness of the heart springs not so much from the breast as from an appeased appetite, that inherent goodliness is but a by-product of a material plenty—and, lo, the virtues of dark souls have been explained away at the snapping of fingers. Strange, this, for on Maupiti, an imperfect South Sea island, neither beau-

tiful nor luxuriant, but poor, humble, and isolated, there was
an over-amount of goodness and hospitality. The six miles of
shore were not overburdened with yams or coconuts. There
was a scarcity of wild pig and goat in the hills, while the lagoon, for all its size, often required a community fish-drive,
so capably described in the late Samuel Russell's *Tahiti and
French Oceania*, to yield even a moderate catch. And yet we
were feasted, first by Tira, who, old though he was, went
into the hills and stuck a pig for the purpose; then by Tu,
who insisted on two pigs; by the ancient man in the hut next
to Piau's; by Tu's mother and the chief; while every family
strove to entertain us, to press on us leis of small flowers, valued beads, shells, rags of *tapa*, offering them not on bended
knees, but carelessly, as though neither they nor the trinkets,
nor even we, to whom they would be kind, were of particular importance. When we sat down to a meal on Piau's veranda the people gathered outside to laugh, to watch our
every action, to coach Farno's sister as she served the food;
perhaps to sing to us, as the sun, in that most quiet hour,
dropped behind the cliffs, and a solution of navy shadow
wavered before our eyes, flooded the lagoon, and masked the
hills and the hazy stretch of ocean. And then, with darkness
coming on, very likely the gramophone would be brought
out, and the people would sit in the crude roadway
charmed, hour after hour, by the three Hawaiian melodies.
Or perhaps a dance would begin under a smoky moon, first
native-fashion, then, to the astonishment and delight of

many of the old people, we ourselves would join, to dance on the cobble and mud with barefooted island girls, so graceful, so strong, so shy. . . . And with daylight laughter was not abandoned. There was little of reproach, few fingers shaken amid an almost holy lack of holiness. . . . The Evening comes so soon, crossing the Dark Lagoon, touching the House. *It* will interfere; *It* will stop laughter. Let no Islander do this, no mortal! . . .

Held weather-bound by high rollers in the pass, we had time to go over much of Maupiti, to see the little lanes of hibiscus trailing through a wood, marking where another village had been. The inhabitants were gone, dead of that far-flung pestilence of European war fields—influenza. Their houses had fallen to the ground, disappeared, and only the flowers of their doorways remained. A yet earlier village was found on the north-western coast, also forsaken, the stone compound and wharf for war-canoes in ruin. During the first quarter-moon it is taboo to walk the old compound, just as it is unwise to show disrespect to the Old Woman who Fell down the Mountain, a huge stone goddess with the face of a hag, lying flat on her back and gazing furiously at the sky. The goddess was a victim of a landslide and the religious fervour of a long-departed missionary, who, to render her impotent, had severed her body in two. But she remains a power—the King of Raiatea broke a palm-frond on her arm and died the same night—and, among other duties, protects the ruined tomb of the last

Maupitian king, in whose vicinity one must never cease moving, lest he be stricken with elephantiasis, a curse from which only the King's descendants are free. I met one on the spot, a young man gathering wood, who in rather superior tones told me that the King had been a man ten feet tall, a god who with one hand could break the hardwood spear of his strongest enemy. I listened seriously, without any desire to point out that the tomb itself was but a thin structure less than six feet overall. Faith and inspired belief are as rare as facts are common.

We climbed the cliffs to hunt tropic birds for the village, armed with the .22 Winchester and a shotgun to back up the rifle should it miss its mark. Ascending to the burial caves where rest the *tapa*-covered bones of the dead, we found the cliffs precipitous and slippery. It was hard to draw a bead. After there had been several close calls Taggart, aiming high, slipped and fell headlong down the cliff. We heard his gun strike the trees and clatter on to stone a good sixty feet below, but, peering over, saw that instead of being with it he was clinging miraculously to the protruding limb of a tree. Rather breathless, his shoulder wrenched, he insisted on climbing back and joining us. Hardly had he done so when, hearing a shout, we turned to see Dombey vanishing from sight, head over heels. Expecting anything, as at this point the cliff was sheer, we hurried down to find him on a ledge thirty feet below. He sat up, rubbed himself, looked cautiously over the edge, felt his arms, his legs, his head, examined the gun he still held, and, mumbling a few words, arose and climbed the cliff again. I wanted to call off the venture, but the stubbornness of the others prevailed, and we ended the day with a heavy catch, divided among the natives.

On the 22nd of May, 1935, we cleared for the atoll of Mopihaa. Only the night before Farno, son of Piau Terope, had asked us in all seriousness not to sail, but to stay in Maupiti, where he and his father and Tu—in fact, the whole village—would build us each a house in which we might live for ever. And now in the morning we were seeing them for the last time, a small band gathered in the age-old shadows of the lava bluffs—Piau Terope; Tu's mother; Tu himself, in a huge green loin-cloth, his loyalty bringing him close to tears; the King's descendant, bowing condescendingly and playing a ukulele of breadfruit rind; and old Tira, standing rather bewildered beside his wife and waving not quite in the proper direction. The sails filled, the motor started, and we set towards the pass, carrying Farno and Gerlac, their canoe towing astern. The people cheered, a humble echo, out of darkness, passing over the unyielding lagoon as the *Cimba*, herself of humble origin, was blown on to lighted water. And out there, on reaching the islets guarding the pass, we took leave of our good friend Farno, and of Gerlac, who for all I know may be in Maupiti to this day.

Dombey coaxed the temperamental engine to perform, Taggart and I dropped sail, leaving it loose for an emergency, saw to it that the anchors were cleared, but stopped against boarding water, after which Taggart took the helm, I the bows. The trail of blue water narrowed between the coral as an outgoing current hurried us into the breach. The engine pumped hard, and the water grew confused, until I could hardly find the channel amid the coral. The centre shoal flashed underneath and fell astern, the eddies increased, the engine drove harder, our course curved, then straightened out. A wave came in, ran the opposing current, tumbled; our bows, forced by the hot engine, cut into the sea, smashed half-way through, only to be driven down by the propeller. A sweep of sea, cabin-high, cleared the decks, flinging me from the jibstay to the foremast. I saw that Taggart was still at the helm, and, getting up, moved back to the bows. The worst was behind, and we rode the tops of two breakers even as the motor tried to screw us beneath them. Just clear of the pass the engine died, and, with a sharp reef immediately to leeward, we rushed the sails into action, to have them lift rather than bury the vital bows.

Alive once more with her sails, the schooner dipped to a crisp wind and swinging sea, clawed off, and reached for Mopihaa, a hundred miles west by south of Maupiti, whose bleak hills grew fainter and fainter, until finally, with the sky red in the west, they were nowhere to be seen. The night came on pleasantly, stiff with wind, as cold as the close-by stars that glittered until the dawn.

SIXTEEN

OCEAN, SUNLIGHT, AND SHADOW

BEFORE SIX of the morning watch we came upon Mopihaa, sometimes known as Mopelia Atoll, sometimes as Lord Howe Island, of the Scilly Group. A circle of reef and islets ridged a ten-mile lagoon, the south-western arc formed by reef alone, the north-western by patches of small islands, the eastern by a long and narrow island curving south for possibly eight miles. The land was low, at little more than reef-level, and seldom attaining an altitude of four feet. Thousands of palms grew down the arm of the eastern island, but nowhere at all was there a visible sign of earth; only coral sand as far as the eye could see.

Scouting the coast, we came upon the boat passage in the north-western reef. Here, instead of seas running into the passage, the flow was outgoing, generated by the prevailing trade lifting a sea over the southern reef, flooding the lagoon, and forcing the water to drain with a rush through the narrow pass.

If the attempt to run the pass was an incautious one the preparations were, on the other hand, of an extremely cautious nature. Almost half an hour passed before the engine was turning over to our satisfaction, the sails lowered and left loosely frapped, the decks tidied, the gear faked down, the anchors catted with stocks shipped and cables shackled to their rings, and the two wingsail booms cleared, ready for poling. But, this done, with Dombey guarding the motor, Taggart in the eyes, myself at the helm, we drove in at our full engine speed of five and a half knots. Progress dropped quickly from two knots to less than two, to less than one, as the schooner, caught in the current, was retarded like a fish working up a freshet. And like a fish she quivered with a growing rigidity against the opposing pressure. Stiffening as though set in concrete, determined to move some way, and unable to move ahead, she suddenly skated cross-keel in an unanticipated lunge on her beam. Steadied just in time, we forced her back into the flow, and pressed on up-water. The pass, while not a long one, was narrow, with a current demanding that we learn right then and there how to offset the wild lunges of the schooner. We answered with these ma-noeuvres. As soon as the craft became rigid in the eye of the outflow we eased her slightly, and then, even as the current struck and forced her to spurt for one side, the helm was thrown over, bringing her about, to run for the other, when again the helm was quickly changed.

With the engine at full speed we made good some fifteen yards in that number of minutes, only to see that the chan-nel ahead was narrowing and floored with shoal. We wanted to put back for safe water. But there was not the room to turn, and the only other solution, to slow engine and ease out sternway, was too dangerous. The old-fashioned motor was likely to fail if at all throttled, to trap us in the coral. Taggart ran for a wing boom, imploring Dombey to "keep that engine talking," and, with the *Cimba* straining for the bottleneck, made ready for poling. The angles of the tacks narrowed, and the current became tighter, rushing over shoal we were relieved to find sunk in fairly deep water. Ar-riving at a point where the coral lay closest to either side, we all at once seemed to trip our keel on solid water. Swerv-ing quickly, cutting a spurt of water with the port bow, the craft staggered cross-stream, reaching quickly through the current. She halted, gained another foot forward—and like a dream rushed on to the calm lagoon.

With the engine silenced and a look-out in the rigging to ward off coral heads we moved under sail to the eastward, finally anchoring in three fathoms off the main shore. Two natives in a brilliantly painted outrigger came alongside, and after a greeting in Tahitian paddled us to the beach, where Charlie Sanford, half-caste overseer, welcomed us. Together with sixteen Tahitians he was marooned for half a year on uninhabited Mopihaa, to gather, split, and dry copra. The Tahitians, isolated from their good island, were quiet, un-demonstrative, as though suffering from some unhappy sickness. After the friendly Charlie Sanford had shown us the three native lean-tos, the cook shack and roofed oven, the cottage and the whitewashed "trade store," we set sail for the islets across the lagoon, promising to return for supper. However, on the way back the wind fell, the engine wouldn't run, and at sunset we were forced to take the pad-dles from a borrowed canoe to paddle the schooner. She moved like a boat, she was so light, but nevertheless it was hard work, and we were glad to sight a whaleboat putting out for us as the flood of the lagoon turned red, the circle of islands solid black. Charlie's men took our hawser, and with good, long sweeps hurried us towards a fire burning on the beach.

Knowing that an atoll can offer little more than coconuts and fish, we brought ashore several valued tins of corned beef, some ship's bread, and a pound of dried prunes. But supper was already prepared, and our host, asking us to sit down, ordered one of the boys to start serving. To our amazement the meal, begun with onion soup, was followed by raw fish, roasted chicken, potatoes, fresh bread, both red and white wines, and Tahitian coffee. Charlie Sanford was an epicure, going to no end of trouble to stock his post, bringing the chickens alive from Tahiti, building an oven that bread might be had daily, and seeing to it that the potatoes and onions were kept well preserved in the sand.

Supper over, we gave a gramophone concert. But for once the machine was a gloomy failure. The older Tahitians went straightway to rest, while the younger ones, after an attempt at cheerfulness, relapsed into wistful states of homesickness. They could not live without laughter and flowers and love, and in vain were the gay pieces played. The wind bullied the metallic sound of the machine; darkness closed in, exaggerated, complete, dwarfing the fire, which grew brighter but smaller, until at an early hour it was kicked apart and buried in the sand.

In the clear sunrise we waded to an island off the main shore, and on the way each of us, unassisted, speared a sand shark with a shaft of limewood. We returned with eggs, seashells, and a pair of small tropic birds, and, scantily clothed against the noon sun, paused a moment in the cool of Mopihaa's graveyard—a little group of rotted stones and ancient boards marking the graves of eight or ten natives, an unknown sea-captain, and a mysterious Swiss baroness, who, it is said, still haunts the shore on moonlight nights. We opened coconuts and drank deeply while looking down the white coast. The *Cimba* was resting. Young palms, vivid and green, swept in one line almost to the horizon, rolling and flashing in a wind that was gone with dramatic suddenness, to leave them hushed, hanging green over the old graves. A fine, undulating rain of sunlight fell through the shadows massed about the trunks. And then once more the wind stirred in the south. The fragile silence was over. Booming, brushing tree-top to tree-top, the gust staggered up the beach before an advancing wave of moving sunlight and shadow, tossing leaves that ripped like silk, sweeping by, salty, flecking the sand, hard running for the misty sea. Again a hollow silence, the coconut leaves strung like coloured glass against the sky; again a wave of thunder, of windblown wood rubbing wood, mingled with the echo of seas on shoal: the sounds of an island—restlessness, utter peace, and the return, ever the return, of restlessness. . . .

We speared fish until dark. The next day Taggart and Dombey, who had become almost inseparable, set off lobstering, while I went six miles down the weather coast searching for the remains of the American sailing-ship *Retriever*, wrecked some thirty years before. Aided by Charlie Sanford, I found a good many clues telling of her end. Fragments of fine whitened cabin moulding two miles beyond the remains of a forehouse indicated that she had broken in two after running ashore, the after-section drifting north. Coal and black stone revealed cargo and ballast, suggesting that she had been on the once popular run from Newcastle, Australia, to San Francisco. We found the cheeks of a topsail halyard block, but, hunt though we would, no trace of the figurehead, last seen in the brush ten years before, could be discovered.

The following day broke with heavy thunderstorms and a low glass, and we spent the time in the cosy cook shed, yarning with Charlie Sanford, playing casino with ancient cards, fortified by a bottle of wine, mild and red, and a heap of Dutch tobacco. There was no change at night, but the sun was out with the morning, allowing us to cross the lagoon to examine the auxiliary sailing-ship *Seeadler*, ex-*Pass of Balmaha*, Count von Luckner's famous raider, our main purpose in calling at Mopihaa. There was little left of her, for she had slipped off the lip of the reef, on which we discovered bits of metal, three rusted tanks, boilers, the twisted doubling of one of her tops, and several four-inch German shell-cases, the factory-marks on the primers ranging from 1909 to 1915. Charlie Sanford, accompanying us, stated that some while back a native schooner had loaded twenty tons of the capped explosives for bilge ballast, carrying them without accident for several years. He also told of one of his boys who, in a mutinous state, dug a hole in the sand, 'aimed' a live projectile at the trading-post, four miles across the lagoon, then heaped a large fire upon it. The shell went off, he assured us, almost blowing up the beach, and the boy with it.

Upon a little island adjacent to the reef we found bits of pine decking, a rotted grating, a spectacle clew, and what must have been one of the *Seeadler's* upper topsail yards, the jack and brace-bands rusted, the parrel gone. Coming upon nothing more, we set about lobstering and catching birds for supper, spending a good night before a windy fire of driftwood.

On the 28th of May we bade our good and friendly host good-bye, and, slipping safely through the boiling pass, set course for the Samoa Islands, nine hundred miles away. Off soundings the *Cimba* jumped to life, and with dead-eyes under worked out to the westward in a smart and brisk manner. Mopihaa disappeared beneath the horizon, grey clouds flew at low altitudes, and tropic birds ranged over the sea, staying their wings against a driving wind. Four-hour watches were set, and, the weather growing, an extra man stood by to shorten down. By nightfall seas were breaking sharply, lightning lit the sky, the south moaned, and the *Cimba*, slim and buoyant, ran with porpoises at her side, lifting to eight knots, steadying to seven, and for minutes on end bettering nine, fast-holding her cloth under a moderate gale.

Just at daybreak the wind backed four points, punched up a cross-sea, and rolled us savagely, affecting the sails winged overside. In pouring rain we decided to drop all canvas in danger of jibbing and set the wingsails. But even as the new gear was dragged on deck a precipitous roll sent us grasping for lifelines and handrails. Then I saw the main boom dig the sea, rise out, ride half-way up the mast, shake crazily in a gust, and, swinging over, hit with full force a thin, taut plough-steel preventer. The sail flogged and collapsed, while the boom, broken in two, dragged in the wash. We hove it on board, belayed it, stowed the sail, and then, in an almost horizontal rainstorm, the wingsails were set for a drive westward. And so into another night, the wind stiff, the sea piling, the schooner trooping, trying hard, pounding, working with her back through every hour.

Fair weather returned in two days, the Pacific became once again blue, white-capped, sleepy-troughed, and we set about repairing the boom, first scarfing and securing it with machine bolts, then fishing the splice with soap-box battens and heavy spun line, finishing the job in lantern-light. With evening the wind veered west, grew stronger, gained high velocity, and caused us to heave-to for the first time in this ocean. Riding snugged-down to the weather—a rather familiar experience for Dombey and me, a long-forgotten one for Taggart—we recognized the signs of a far-reaching disturbance, one originating perhaps in the forties or fifties, possibly from a Southerly Duster in the latitudes of New Zealand.

The storm died. Cat's-paws and light, unreliable trades set in. For days we moved under dry, remote skies, through the

slow, drugged hours of flying-fish weather, through passion-
less, quiet nights. At times the schooner limped with the
patched boom; at times she sent a happy wash over-
shoulder; or she would falter as strange breezes glided from
beam to beam, twisted over a flat sea, and vanished into
space. We would regard her with disparagement, compas-
sion, ill-humour; patience, reverence, intolerance. She was
the pivot of action to each of our lives. Nothing on ten thousand miles of water was so important. We knew her every
weakness, the last ounce of her strength, her will, her small
failings, jaunty enthusiasms, her occasional melancholy—
and concerned ourselves primarily with her destiny.

The testing of a craft goes on for ever—there is no end
to it—but a point is reached where finally the spirits of ship
and men to some degree reflect each other, where often the
weakness of one becomes the weakness of the other, the
strength of one the other's strength.

A makeshift craft will not do. Long-voyage crews are influenced above all by the temperament of the boat they sail,
adjusting themselves to her living spirit. That a cruiser can
be but a machine-like convenience for reaching new and al-
luring lands is an illusion. She must be more. She must live,
and she must be made to live. She must have the character,
the turn of temperament, the high spirit, to dwell in salt
water, with the flow of a wave, with something of the wind,
captured in her own bones. Perhaps all things touching the
elements so completely must have this conforming character

and this flame in order to exist. At any rate, once off soundings the sea can make or break the spirit of any venture by
making or breaking the spirit of the craft, and in turn that of
the crew. The craft herself must also be an adventurer in the
real sense—a living spirit. And that spirit is more vital than
vague, emanating in a good craft directly from the integral
spirit of her designer; a symbol revealing his science, but,
more important, his art, and even before these his ideals,
loyalties, faiths. And there is nothing mystical here; for those
contemplating a voyage merely a hint that the craft chosen
be approved by the heart as well as by the mind, that she be
designed by one who goes beyond to the feel of ships, striving to find Truth in his creation, not by one who is a scientist only, and, lastly, never by a layman, for never yet has a
happy home-designed cruiser sailed the seas.

Dombey, Taggart, and I, despite our poor start, came to
work satisfactorily together. The one solid bunk, along with
a collapsible one, sufficed; there was an extra hand for tight
weather, and short four-hour watches for us all. But perhaps a three-man crew is not an ideal combination. Two
may side against one, destroying the delicate balance of the
unit, a balance that once lost is seldom retrieved. Then one
may see a thing one way, a million men may see it exactly
the same, but almost invariably three will see it differently.
And, again, a vessel that may be handled by two should not
have a third, for there should be nothing superfluous, left
over, unused—not even man-power.

Over-manning may easily ruin a voyage. A crew demoralized by idleness lose the zest of the venture, and often dissipate the fine sea-watches with noise, lending confusion where silence is a virtue. Over-manning happens most often, I think, in the large fifty- and sixty-footers, and it is interesting to note how little their sea life resembles that offered by a smaller cruiser. The difference of a foot or two, a ton or two, changes the very nature of a voyage. Perhaps aboard a craft of the *Cimba's* size the ocean appears more forceful, pugnacious, inspiring. At any rate, I have seen more than one large cruiser come in with a crew of four or six, seven or eight, so unimpressed by what they were leaving behind that they might have been travelling first-class. But different ships different long splices, as they say. These same crews would swarm the beach, fresh and vigorous, not like hollow-eyed ghosts come off some fantastic ocean with a hitch in their belts, but ready to wrestle from the shore everything exciting, refreshing, instructive. And so it is: the large cruiser very often finds highest adventure in the new port, the small one on the sea.

The wind, one hour rolling a sharp chop, would be gone the next. A squall would bear down, wild with rain, bluster by, dragging over a silent sea, and long periods of calm would follow. The sky, yellow behind empty horizons; waterspouts and heated, leaden clouds forming over seas barren even of driftwood; and weak trails of sunlight, leading now east, now west, to the decline of a swollen sun. The sails flogging, in cyclonic airs, hanging limp, or stretched beneath clouds of uncertain colour, of no shape at all.

On the seventh day out from Mopihaa the sky was blown clear, the sun shone in earnest, and the ocean became once more brilliant, blue with light.

One peaceful afternoon, with all well and the nearest land reckoned some distance off, I was alarmed at the helm by a sudden sound, not unlike that of a small surf. The *Cimba* was swaggering before a south-easter at the time, a pair of wingsails poled out before her like old-fashioned studding-sails, blocking the view beyond the bows. Peering beneath them, I saw something awash, a dark form, hardly forty feet away, and immediately in our path. A reef? I flung the helm to port, but the sails were slow spilling wind, and the schooner closed in. Bringing the tiller amidship, I again hove it to port. But the obstacle began to move, to gather way, lunging on the sea. In came the *Cimba*, smoking, heaving for all she was worth. There was a loud splash. We grazed by, and I turned to see a whale, a great sulphur bottom, awakened from sleep and beginning to sound, its tremendous black tail sliding into the ocean like a bad dream.

Held in the chains of a two-knot current, slowed by headwinds, we finally came upon the island of Tau, Star of Samoa, dim under the scudding mist of a vast moonlit squall. We hove-to until dawn, then, nine days some hours out from Mopihaa, sailed for the high coast. Landing on a sunny beach, decorated by the finest carved canoes any of us

had encountered, we explored the village of Loma, a group
of symmetrical open houses artistically constructed of hardwood pillars and yellow pandanus roofs. The only white
man on Tau, Chief J. Sommers, U.S. Navy, greeted us
warmly, and, together with his charming wife, set about
making the unexpected event of visitors a pleasant one. Mrs
Sommers insisted on preparing a lunch, at which I fear we
shamed ourselves, having recently come upon lean times that
allowed but one meal a day. We did not like the natives. A
serious thing, running down a thousand miles to fetch a
land for which one has no taste! These people had been seriously pampered, not by Sommers, but by official commissions and their impersonal philanthropy. For the first time
since leaving Panama natives boarded the *Cimba* uninvited,
jabbered almost aggressively. The younger generation were
schooled in the equal rights of man, in English and American history, and in the values of material assets they can
never possess. They are intelligent, yet no brighter than the
Polynesians, and, finally, they are quite sophisticated, as this
letter to Chief Sommers, inviting us to a feast, amusingly re-
veals:

June 7, 1935

DEAR SOMMER,

I am asking your honour, if you do wish to let the gentlemen welcome to my residence, I believe you are so anxious to
hold them there, however excuse me in that way.

I want to represent a personal reception as in the Samoan
custom, and I have already prepared food for themself. I believe they are all your Aigas [friends] it is because gentlemen

from New York, but you with Mrs Sommer is my aiga. So, whatever I have been doing for them are yours

I am going to prepare some entertainment to amuse the gentlemen, Sivasiva [dance] hoping you'll be done with benefience

Yours trueley
NUA

Let them come with that bearer if you willing. Dont get bother I'll do my best to look after what be happen.

Perhaps the strangest thing about the letter is the mention of New York. Natives all over the Pacific will speak of 'Frisco—a high island without a lagoon and lacking coconut-trees—but not before or since have I encountered one who had even heard of New York. Well, we went to the feast, sipped ceremonial kava, watched beautiful Samoan dancers, and upon the insistence of the people found it in us to follow in the steps of the departed commissions with three long speeches. The talks for some reason impressed the villagers, who set about treating us nobly—and while they were doing so some of them broached the *Cimba's* locks, to make off with the last of our rations. The theft, also the first since Panama, was quickly discovered, and most of the goods regained, but thereafter a close watch was kept. Finally we got under way for Pago Pago, west by south seventy miles, having as guests the high chief Tufale, officially known as Governor of Manua, besides Tooa, a young Samoan, the ninth and tenth native passengers carried by the *Cimba*.

The run was made in moonlight before a warm night wind that tracked the sea and hurried the *Cimba*, until she flew under a wide sky, as though on her trial trip, the gear humming, her paintwork and sails growing blue under the moon. I was keeping her for invisible Tuituila Island when Tufale, the chief, ponderous, pompous in a purple *lava lava*, came and rested on the after-cabin top.

"I do not blame you," he said in good English, his eyes on the schooner. "I do not blame you sailing even for so long."

All Islanders are seamen at heart; all seamen incline towards islands.

"Come steer a while. See what you can do."

He climbed into the well and, holding the tiller gently, concentrated on the dipping bows. For a moment he was silent, then, without looking up, asked, "Tufale will take the ship until to-morrow?"

But that was hardly to be, for although Tau had not been left until sunset, the *Cimba* was off Tuituila before three in the morning, to be hove-to until light. Then, in the early dawn, with Dombey at the helm, she came into the dark harbour of Pago Pago, anchoring off the Naval Station.

Pago Pago! Shadows of mountains over-riding the dead-rotted jungle! . . . The thirty days of rain. Bored, miserable, unhappy naval officers; pampered, restless natives. The vicious and unprovoked ramming of native hardwood canoes against the hull, and minor warfare with fists, paddles, wing-sail booms. The *Cimba* looted once more; and unmoved naval authorities revealing their inability to provide at any cost the replacements of stolen charts; their refusal to sell at any price the lumber for a new boom. The three of us, not always fully fed, biding time, sitting patiently in the cabin, listening to the rain, waiting, waiting, for the mail-steamer and funds, weeks away. The arrival of a cruising boat called *Igdrazil*, manned by a nautical couple; the silent nights spent hauling out their boat on the full of the tide. The leave-taking with Dombey.

"Dombey" Russell Dickinson, capable at sea, admired in every port of call, left almost as nonchalantly as he joined. Not really so: the trust we had endeavoured to hold would not allow for that. For nearly two years he and I had sailed shoulder to shoulder—something of a record, I believe, among unpaid crews—and in that time he had taken much of the responsibility, the good with the bad, tending to the needs of the craft, withstanding what he would call my "poetic doldrums" ashore, my "clipper-ship fashions" at sea. And by now I knew the reason for his leaving: it was to take up a greater trust. Dombey was bound for home and marriage. He left us as an officer of an Hawaiian-bound four-master, destined to meet with her last adventure. Strange we come so close to men, we move on so far together, over valleys, seas, sharing illusory victories against time and space, suddenly to be parted, to wonder each in his own heart whether he is not for ever alone upon the width and the breadth and the depths of his own, his unsharable world.

Early on the 11th of July the *Cimba* cleared Pago Pago, and, lifted by a swift sea, sailed yet farther west for Apia, British Samoa. The new boom, turned down from a piece of lumber through necessity bought from a British trader on American land, worked well, and under the sunny canvas Taggart and I once more felt a peace, a peace that not even the arch of a red squall, striking off Saleaaumua Road, could disturb, and happily we rolled into Apia Harbour, making a flying moor off the Customs shed, to learn some surprising news from Pago Pago. The Navy had recommended the crew of the *Cimba* to the officials of British Samoa!

The town of Apia has not changed greatly since the days of Robert Louis Stevenson; a few more buildings, perhaps a little less trade, the Germans gone, the New Zealand Commission reigning. The harbour, lying between Vaitela and Fagalu bays, on the north coast of the island of Upolu, is barricaded by shoal, the shore protected by a long retaining wall built just beyond the rusted skeleton of the German warship *Adler*, lost in the hurricane of 1889. The town—a small form under the hill ranges—is quiet, sunny, out-of-the-way; the people, colonial, friendly, a few of them remembering Stevenson. A Mr King, who went to England to settle the writer's estate, had found him "a very fine gentleman—very kind, and funny at times." An ancient trader in a great Island hat banded with yellow sea-shells shook his head. "A dreamer!" he exclaimed. "Mr Stevenson— 'Tusitala,' they would call him—should have kept clear of

Samoan politics. There were two sides at the time—and both of them wrong. Help the poor natives, hey? These people ain't Tahitians, you know. Why, every last one of them is a born politician as wouldn't be set without an opposing party! Pacific Ocean Irishmen, we name 'em." And another old man recalled him as being "naturally a good colonist, with many possibilities."

The *Cimba* was hove down on her bilge, scraped, painted, floated, and anchored off the customs wharf. We laid aboard water and a few supplies for a voyage to the Fiji Islands.

On our final day in Polynesia we climbed the top of the mountain of Vaea to find Stevenson's grave. It was a simple mould of concrete almost lost in weed and myrtle, and marked by a weathered plaque. The sun at the time had almost disappeared; only a golden line, thin and ruling the edge of a calm sea, shone in the west. The mountains were dark, heavy, leaning on the fragile base of bays and the diminutive capes far below. Floods of perpendicular shadow fell from the peak of Vaea, dropped through forests burdened by parasites, and came to brood over a river and its tributaries, which, like so much tarnished thread, wove in dull silver through the jungle, passed Vailima, curved a few times, and disappeared. There was utter silence between clouded sky and ocean, and not a thing stirred. Then a horizon cloud parted, to be blown into thin air, and for a moment the sun, red and windy, brightened the sea, lit a treetop, a peak, a cliff of flowers, the brush at our feet, the last two lines cut on the simple grave:

> Home is the sailor, home from sea,
> And the hunter home from the hill.

And suddenly out of the sun came a wind to shake the jungle, to move like a half-smothered surf up the river valley. Reddened light burned into the darkness, into the cold inclined recesses of trees, until the entire highland flared in shifty light. The wind boomed, the narrow peak seemed to sway, and all at once we fancied that we caught a foreboding note in the wild air. But then the sun dropped and the land became silent, lethargic in clear twilight.

SEVENTEEN

THROUGH THE KORO SEA

JULY 27TH. After we had been towed to sea by the accommodating pilot cutter sail was set, and we put astern a three-masted schooner belonging to the London Missionary Society, passed the large trader *Makoa*, of the Burns Philp South Seas Company, and footed for Apolina Strait, reaching that point at four o'clock, when departure for Suva, Fiji, was taken from an islet waving five palms and called Nuu Lea Lea; then Upolu and the volcanic steps of Savaii, the sister island, dropped to a widening ocean.

The first part of the trip, roughly five hundred sailing miles over deep water to Nanuku Passage, which breaches the Koro Sea, was run upon the northern extremity of the south-east trades. Until midway along this first leg, when Good Hope Island appeared, Taggart was sufficiently ill to be confined below; however, as I was accustomed to rather long watches, and as the *Cimba* was by nature a one-man craft, work was carried on very much as usual.

Our methods of navigation had been simple throughout: an early-morning sight, another at noon, a postmeridian every so often, an exmeridian, only an occasional Sumner line, while on the entire voyage but a single star sight had been taken, the economy of sextant work being bolstered by developing a skill in dead reckoning. Bowditch longitude tables had been first replaced by those of Dreisenstok, later by Agerton's, and we were considering changing again, to Martelli's short method—the greater possible error to be compensated for by the mean of a larger number of equations. However, beyond piloting and aiding in dead reckoning, I did little or none of the navigating, which first Dombey, then Taggart, managed so capably.

With Taggart once more on deck, we hung becalmed as Good Hope, an isolated island of the kingdom of Tonga, appeared in the silent offing. There was not a sound from sea or sky for two days. The schooner swayed only when we moved within her; her sails were dropped; an awning was spread over the deck, and we waited for wind on the cabin-tops. The calm stretched wearily into distance. We thought we saw mirages upon the horizons, and all day long the sun fell from hot, vacant skies, brutally blue. Sharks swarmed round the hull, threw their heads into the glare, and rubbed them against the stern—a splash, a cushioned blow against the hull, a momentary glimpse of a grey, vicious-eyed head. It was incredible! The cabins echoed as they rammed us. We hit them with wing booms, and when that had no ef-fect left them to their weird sport until they drew off, and Good Hope, itself a mirage, floated into the west, some-where between sky and sea, and held there.

Finally, like a living breath, a north-west wind began to blow. The awning was housed, the sails were swung up the naked masts, and the white schooner plunged again, shook us, and ripped a thin wake with her narrow sides. Passing to the south of Zephyr Shoals, she swung west two hun-dred miles, then, on picking up Wailangilailai Light, under the boilers of Duff Reef, began a long leg down the Koro Sea. Lighted by strong sunshine, she scudded for Suva before high winds, her spoon driving, her sails heaving shadows over a running flame of spume; over the yellow decks, the rigging, the black anchors lashed to deck-chocks. Island af-ter island appeared in the intense sea-light: Tavenui, the

Ring Golds, Kanathea, and Naitamba—all of the great Fiji group. At sundown we sighted the old Sandalwood Coast of Vanua Leva, a mystery in bronze mountains. And so into the dark, crossing the 180th meridian in the middle watch.

It was on that night that we carried all sail for Horseshoe Reef, unaware that a Norwegian freighter had shortly before run aground, to jettison immense hardwood logs still floating on the dark sea. But we ran without incident until morning, when, passing Nairai and Ngau, we stood in for Viti Levu, principal island of Fiji, striving against a dying wind to fetch Suva by sunset. But the dead wind veered south, tightened, blew up a crushing slop, and we spent the night snugged down in the rain, feeling into a moderate gale for a lee under Astrolabe Lagoon, reached some time in the graveyard watch. Rainstorms, thunder, a pitching sea throughout. Then calm, with a red dawn lighting the decks and the tight wet sails.

We steered north thirty miles, and with the house flag and now fading ensign at the trucks came into Suva ten days out of Apia, rounding up under the hulk of the old wind-jammer *Woodburn*, to find a berth amid the native shipping off the town. We looked over-harbour. To the west of the channel, where the wreck of the iron barque *Norden* lay on shoal, the sky was filled with mountains; to the east the steeply banked town reared in a more or less compact wave of whitewash and red roof-paint, eventually giving way to the green, interesting hills of the district of Lami. The native ships, plumb-stemmed after the British, black, heavy of spars, were moored just beyond a large modern wharf, built on reclaimed ground under the town. A group of little yachts swung at their tackle. The Grand Pacific Hotel, resembling some vast summer palace of the East, loomed over the waterfront. Beyond the royal palms and weeping fig-trees of the Botanical Gardens and Government grounds grew to the edge of a shoreline curving for Suva Point. On the other side of the wharf were machine shops, the Public Works Slip, an oil dock, the cool trees shading the magical rivers of Lami.

We went ashore, strolling along Victoria Parade, a white street, arcaded, clean, the shops fluttering bright awnings in the wind. The pathways were filled with well-attired Europeans, traders, clerks, prospectors; happy, pomp-headed Fijians; shirt-tailed Indians, Sikh police in puttees and brave of turbans—the British Colonial scene at its best. Passing over a little bridge, we entered the shade of All Nations Street, to be first surrounded, then lost, in the crowd: bare-footed Fijians in *sulus*, some in scarlet coats; admirable Rotumahs, Britishers; stately Punjabees, Moslems, Bombayese, Madrassis, in turbans, in shawls, in grey, brown rags. The air under the shadowy walls was heavy, stale with the odours of coco-oils and incense, opium and steamed spices, flat bread and sweet, over-ripe fruit. There was the clamour of slippery, unintelligible tongues, and soft undertones—the half-heard chants of Eastern beggars—chants that would go on far into the night as they touched the gowns, the passing shawls, of a walled-in humanity. Climbing Waimanu Road, we saw the harbour sheeted calm under brown mountains of unpronounceable name that lifted to the sky like the misted hills of a Chinese print. On the waterfront we had bread and butter and tea at a little shop, the Black Cat, after which we bought a sixpenny packet of cigarettes, half a pound of tobacco, a side of veal, and punted back to the *Cimba*.

For a month we awaited the mail-steamer and a cheque from the *Rudder* magazine, and for a month it rained, as circular draughts lunged cross-bay, heavy with a vegetable musk of damp coco-plants and rubber-trees. We lived on pennies, bartering much of the while with odd shirts and mildewed shoes, trying to put by as we did so for a trek out to the Solomons and the New Guinea north coast. Taggart was the genius behind these operations. The George Taggart of Afghanistan, Siberia, and the Yukon, of the priceless moustache, his tall straw hat raked acockbill close to one eye, would break the bartering hearts of the market Indians, bargaining halfpenny for halfpenny in their own dialects. Time passed slowly; the *Cimba* rolled quietly, ready for the next move.

Once in a while a freighter would come alongside the wharf. We could hear her winches grinding above the rain, and of a night see her metal skeleton-work angular and stiff against the lights of Suva. One I recognized as a sister-ship to a steamer I had served as A.B. at the happy age of eighteen.

An English warship called. The officers paid us a visit, generously admired the schooner, and told us that the *La Korrigane* had cleared New Zealand for our hoped-for rendezvous at Singapore. When the naval vessel departed, her whistles screaming in the downpour, we decided to leave Suva to spend a week off less rainy islands close by, and there dry out for the voyage ahead. So on one day in early September we got under way for the Kandavu Group, forty miles due south, carrying a borrowed tender over the stern, small amounts of trade tobacco, kava root, and two guests, young men of the town, to ease that inevitable strain known at close quarters, which Taggart and I had been feeling for some while past.

Rain in the South Seas is by no means as frequent as would appear. Only the windward coasts of certain mountainous groups, capable of gathering moisture, are seriously troubled, while the sea, the leeward lands of the same islands, and the majority of low islands are usually bright and clear. A mile or so off the weather shore of Viti Levu the rains cleared, the sun burned on the sea, and we ran south, reaching into an exciting wind, fetching Great Astrolabe Lagoon, green with the small islands of Vanua Kulo, Nevavuni, Ono, and their uninhabited sisters. The sun set over the ocean, but not before we were at anchors, and had thrown up a lean-to of woven palm-fronds on the beach of an island.

Each day we fished, sunrise to sunset, tacking over the

lagoon, a trolling-line astern, a man in the mast-top looking out for coral heads and schools; and each night we camped on a new island or lay at anchors off a new village to drink kava with the chiefs or to smoke with them the coarse Island tobacco wrapped in banana leafing. The days were warm, blue with coral water. The immense palms of the islands soughed, rolled in sunlight, or hung like lighted cut glass against the sky. Nights brought moonlight, washing the beaches white, causing the schooner's masts to glisten, revealing the ocean out to the horizons, catching the forms of little flowers, wild and blowing over seaweed. There would be long evenings of song, and of dancing to the warm noise of skin drums and tom-toms; of long moonlight swims; or they would be quiet ones, the calm of the lagoon unbroken by a sound, the mysterious lands as silent as death.

The week ended finding the schooner in better condition, ready to return to Suva, and we swung on board after a last feast, better in health, confident, and prepared for come what might. With the anchors tended for the night, we left a hurricane lamp burning at the jibstay and turned in. A wind came off sea, smoked the lamp, blew through the trees of Kandavu Island—a wild draught, foreboding, again foreboding.

EIGHTEEN

THE WRECK OF THE CIMBA

AT SIX IN the morning we made sail for Suva, the schooner heaving into light airs with the studied rhythms of a big ship slow-beating up the wind. With Veti Levu in sight faint ghosts stirred from the south-east, passed, and the southern sky became cross-feathered by cirro-cumulus cloud; the headlands darkened under more compact formations, until mountain ranges shone a violent green under walls of black, hanging thunderclouds. The scene lightened, the sun glowed weakly, and, expecting an east wind, we stood in that direction to avoid a beat through Suva Pass. Some rain rattled on the ocean, blew off; the sun dropped, the twilight passed, and a long swell rolled in from the south.

In the dark the east wind began to blow, and we worked into its eye, crawling at perhaps two knots. At ten o'clock the Suva beacon and harbour range light were raised, but as the wind swung to the north-east we kept hacking east to gain weathering before running the passage. We asked our passengers, young Gordon Griffen and Hugh La Forrest, to go below until we were clear. Shortly after speed dropped, and it was almost one in the morning before the schooner had run out the required distance. Coming about quietly, we steered for Suva, eight miles off, the wind now spinning from the north. We took ample bearings on Nasalai Light, as well as on the harbour beacons slowly drawing in line, as for the first time on these seas we navigated with the aid of more than one lighthouse revealing an exact position. With Suva five miles off and the Great Suva Reef two to the north, it began to rain. Thunder sounded on the coast, and the ship was set about by a downpour, a solid wall between shore and sea, a torrential cloudburst cutting off the land wind, the loom of the lights. Suva was abandoned, and we felt south of west for sea-room.

Leaving the steering-well, Taggart and I took up on the sheets sagging overside, then went to the main rigging to watch for a change. Nothing sounded above the noise of the rain. The sails could not shift the hull, and the engine, repaired no fewer than nine times since Tahiti, was definitely silenced. While sensing no particular danger, we were aroused by the craft's helplessness, and felt of the anchors, to make sure that they were clear, knowing as we did so that the coast was sheer, with the hundred-fathom curve immediately off the reef. When an hour of watch had gone by Taggart, shouting something above the noise, disappeared below to look at the chart. I left the shrouds and stood on the storehouse top, just forward of the helm. The compass, shining through the wet deadlight at my feet, indicated that we still headed for sea.

At approximately two-thirty I thought I heard a sound above the rain coming from astern. I looked over the sea, my eyes peering to the edge of a circle of visibility perhaps ten feet through. The downpour was deafening, solid. The sound did not return. But as I wiped the rain from my eyes I saw the ghost of foam.

I moved for the anchors and was passing the mainmast when the ship struck on reef. The deck dropped underfoot, the fore-boom drove against my shoulder—and I had fallen through the companion and on to Taggart, sprawled over the chart. There was a loud roar; the cabin heeled, a barrelful of sea foamed over the hatchway, and in one heap the sleeping passengers, bunk-boards, blankets, and gear fell to pin us underneath. The sound of coral ripping the underbody followed. There was a deafening concussion, and as the hull skidded over shoal I found the companion and made the deck, the others behind. But there was no deck left—only a steep incline piling out of the surf. The sails were in the sea, the lee rigging under, the nearest land two miles off.

We swarmed forward, gripping to the weather rail, up-and-down over our heads. A breaker lifted; there came the cry of "Hold on!" and it pitched against the side, thundered, and drove us through white surf. I reached the fifty-five-pound bower, but young Griffen, who was heavier, took it and threw it perhaps farther than any other anchor has been thrown. Griffen fell in the sea. Two of us got him. I had La Forrest climb into the cabin and see that all lights were out. He returned; nothing was on fire, but, "She's filling." As a slight wind began to blow the seventy-five pounder was made ready, its cable hauled out of the wash and laid in bights over the horizontal foremast. Darkness bound sea and ship, the rain increased, the surf sucked, riding up the sides. All halyards were cast off, the sails being hove down the masts on the run, to offset the broadside of wind. Five times an attempt was made to kedge the anchor out to windward. It could not be accomplished in that sea. We managed to parcel the cable of the smaller hook, which, cutting a twenty-yard groove through the coral, had yet to part.

A heavy breaker swept the rail, forcing us into the masts. The hull vibrated; the rigging clattered. We had done what we could for the craft, and it was time to consider our guests. A dash to leeward might be made in the small tender, too fragile to face the surf. The sea would be quieter under the lee of the reef, where a run for the land could be started. Griffen and La Forrest made ready. We shouted in their ears to send a tugboat—a Government tug, not one demanding immediate salvage. Strange how we insisted on a future even while aware that not one of the craft belonging to the five hundred souls drowned by the reef had got off! Gordon

Griffen, a good young boy, wrung my hand savagely, and he and La Forrest were away. "Good luck!" some one shouted.

An explosion of surf raked the schooner, drowning her in spray. She yanked at her hook, and, together with the anchor, gave way into the coral. After some effort the manilla cable, sweated steel-tight, was parcelled with additional chafing gear where it bit the chock. Then, in silence, Taggart and I struggled to get sails and booms out of the wash and secured with heavy lashing to handrails, now serving as footwalks. The rain eased, and we looked at the black sea, colder than before, and whipped by a drive of wind. There was nothing in sight. The starboard side of the hull lay under water; the port was taking the brunt of the riding sea; however, influenced by the anchor, the hull, which had struck almost broadside, was beginning to point into the waves.

An examination below decks was started on finding a watertight matchbox with which to light the lamp, which, with chimney gone, showed the cabin in ruin, the starboard side submerged, the port so high in the air that we stood with water to our knees, not on the flooring, but on the starboard locker shelves. Two tin boxes, one floating some of Taggart's gear, the other ship's paper, were thrown into a dry locker, holding the chronometer and sextant. Armed with a hurricane lantern, we worked down into the storeroom to find the engine, a thousand rounds of ammunition, and the tanks submerged by a rolling sea, heavy with oil and floating the best part of a hundred charts. As the skin between cabins and planking had not been broached no leaks could be discovered. We threw off the costly weather coats recently presented by a moving-picture company, and, bared to the waist, set about with buckets and five-gallon tins to bail ship. More than once we were flung to our knees by the twisting of the hull, but for fifteen, twenty minutes worked with a will, only to discover in the end that no matter what we did the water reached sea-level. Quite suddenly the cabin made a heavy lunge to leeward, the light went out, and we found ourselves under the slop, hemmed against the bulkheads. The anchor had finally parted!

We were on deck again, laying out the last hook—although we scarcely knew how it was to be done. Because this anchor had been too heavy to cast far enough for a purchase it had been kept aboard. Now we must attempt to make it hold. While paying it over the bow the wet wind strengthened from the ocean. Climbing down the sloping deck, Taggart and I gripped arms and slowly lowered ourselves into the sea. The wash, waist-high, was powerful, and several minutes passed before we were under the bows, feeling for the anchor. Each man lifting a fluke, we began a slow march out to windward, where the grapple might take a hold. The rain closed in. More than once we were put head-under, while one wave set us swimming. We turned to see how it would hit the craft. She rolled down until her mast-tops seemed to strike water, then, as a hard pull was felt on the cable, she disappeared. Throwing a fluke into a pocket of coral, we groped in the sea for the cable, and on holding to it were swept to leeward, where finally the hull loomed out of the darkness. We gained it, and, swinging aboard, took up on the line, belaying it to the foremast foot with a round turn and two half-hitches.

It was almost four o'clock when the smoky lamp below was relit. The grounding had occurred at about two-thirty, and since then we had pounded—literally so—over fifty yards of coral. There was no chance of slipping off the lee edge, for at this point the reef was a mile through. And now a new danger was arising: the tide, which had been steadily retreating, cushioned the effect of the rollers less and less, and the hull, picked up by breakers rushing to leeward, was being left to fall solidly on to rock. It seemed that a total breaking up must shortly take place. A tin of flares was fetched from the ruin in the eyes. A lighted flare might bring aid—but perhaps only the aid of commercial wreckers. Again the insistence on a future—a gesture I had admired in Carrol, in Warren, in Dombey, and now beheld in George Taggart, as throughout the entire night we worked side by side, sharing the best with the worst. The cabin rocked and echoed with the hollow sound of choking water; the ship's bell tolled, and the yellow lamp sent waves of shadows touching the wet brow, the half-submerged and glorious hair of Miss Landi, and the white spars of our old namesake, sailing upside-down on the port bulkhead. Under the dark water were the stoves, the chart table, and, floating above them, fragments of books, charts, papers. A paper suitcase dissolved, and I saw for the last time my sentimental poems, washed page by page into the oblivion beyond the hatch. I felt no regret. We cannot hold the same poetry throughout life. There must ever be change, slow or sudden—a change that breaks as one wild wave, or as a slow tide covering over that which is endeared, which even as we love we lose.

The tide had turned, but we were still hanging on when the light broke. The headland was seen some two miles away, separated from the wide reef by the breadth of Lauthala Water. The schooner lay on a sharp heel sixty yards from the open sea to the south, and the anchor—we had surged the cable at the mast throughout—still gripped. There was no sign of aid, and we grew apprehensive for our passengers.

At six o'clock the pilot cutter *Mona* drew up on the weather side of the reef, launched a surf boat, and Port Captain Nysmyth boarded us. Ways and means of getting clear were considered. The Captain explained the current that had grounded us during the calm as a freak only occasionally setting into Lauthala Water, rare enough to be omitted by all pilot directions, sudden enough to have been nonexistent before the rains came at one o'clock, but strong enough to have set many craft, both local and foreign, on to the reef. During the past fifty years not one of these vessels had got off, each one being destroyed, the longest to last being a crack American schooner, a four-master with six-inch planking, which had survived the surf eight hours before breaking up. We suggested chopping out the masts, unshipping the iron keel, and working her off the lee, but Captain Nysmyth shook his head, declaring it impracticable. After we had declined his offer to board the cutter, being both a true sailor and a gentleman, he set out for Suva to get a tug.

At seven a large white canoe came over the lee. Its owner very kindly took our chronometer and sextant, and told of the night creating a hero. It seemed that after leaving us Griffen and La Forrest were snagged in coral—rotted areas infested with octopus and water-snakes—gashing their feet badly as they waded for Lauthala Harbour. Before long La Forrest severed a tendon, and for a full quarter of a mile young Gordon carried him on his shoulders, while still towing the dinghy. On reaching open water the nearly unconscious La Forrest fell into the tender, breaking one of the two-foot oars. With the oar patched, Griffen worked for more than an hour before the tender struck mud, when again, with the other on his back, he waded a full quarter of a mile. On reaching dry land he made La Forrest as comfortable as possible, then ran for almost a mile to the nearest plantation, reporting us shortly before dawn.

With the sea rising Taggart and I, by using the fore-gaff and a wing boom for heavers, tried working a tarpaulin under the stove-in starboard bilges. But the battered side, pounding on shoal, could not be lifted. At nine-thirty we hove the hawser of Government towboat *No. 6*, the most powerful tug in the waters, through the surf and bent it to the mainmast. The tug opened up at full speed, but the hull did not move. We signalled to ease off, and bent the tow-line through the propeller aperture to obtain a fairer lead. The tug changed direction to break the groove of the keel. Finally the hull moved a foot—a yard—and just then the hawser parted midway. Five times a boat was swamped before a new six-inch manilla had been made fast, and the tug could pull once more. A silent mob gathered at her bitts, watching her strain the tow-rope to breaking-point as she strove to move us. But it was a vain struggle. The tide had been lost; and in the end the line was cast off. "That's the finish!" some one exclaimed.

"We'll try on to-morrow's tide," said Captain Nysmyth. "Get all valuables off, though, I advise." He turned to the owner of the white canoe. "Mr Turner, will you see these two boys ashore before they pass out? Make them take it easy."

At a big house by the sea, where we could view the craft, we had the first meal since leaving Kandavu, having anticipated a large one upon arriving at Suva, and telephoned time and again to make sure of the aid of *No. 6* on the following day. We went back to work, and, aided by the crews of the *Sigawale* and the New Zealander *Arethusa*, our old mooring mates of Suva, strapped eight empty oil-drums under the bilges, to buoy the schooner against the morning tide. The men worked with a will, not one believing that there would be any morning. Even if there was, where was the craft that could be hauled by a tow-boat over sixty yards of reef without losing her bottom? Already she had outlasted the big American by some hours. Night was closing; the breakers were building. The hull was stripped of sails and tackle; the anchor was set out farther, the parted tow-rope serving as a new cable. Companions were battened down, the fore-hatch muzzled with a canvas hood, and then in a wilderness of sunset the men, laughing good-naturedly, carried us bodily away.

Dawn showed the sea bursting, the hull standing, doggedly opposing it. We were on board in short order. The news reached Suva. *No. 6*, manned by thirty volunteers, skippered by Captain Nysmyth himself, steamed out. The Boys' Grammar School declared a holiday to aid us, the Sea Scouts appeared in the old champion *Heather*, and members of a yacht club, who needed every day's pay, appeared on the scene, joined by the crew of a Polish yawl we had known in Panama. With a little cluster of shipping under our lee and the faithful *No. 6* out to windward, we made ready for a last attempt. The tug started, ten or twelve men heaved on either side of the crippled hull, but at the end of half an hour not even a foot had been gained. The tide began to change. During a pause the oil-drums were driven lower into the sea, the masts hove down by a whip leading from the main truck to a kedge. Once more the tug opened up at full, while the crowd swarmed under the bilges. Suddenly we moved, ever so little. There was a sound of crushing coral; a roller came in, driving the men from the sides; but they came back, shouting, heaving. The hull staggered again. Never letting up, the tug strained the hawser bar-taut, the schooner vibrated, moved slowly, pounding towards the surf-line, crushing rock every yard of the way. The spars began to righten, and both rails came flush with the sea as she lifted and crashed a way for open water. At the lip of the reef Taggart and I climbed on board, calling for volunteer bailers. Every one offered; many had to be kept back. The hull dived through the tower of a comber, slumped back, and then with a final pitch lunged on to the sea.

The two of us in the cabin, our heads just clear of the water beneath the carlings, began bailing to keep the craft afloat. The youngsters of the yacht club broached a way into the cabins and, fresh and full of vigour, relieved us of the big oil-cans and set to work like Trojans. At either cabin they worked, two men to a tin, slinging the cans on deck, where another two emptied them, threw them back. Gordon Griffen, his legs in bandages and smiling through tears, was one of them. They began to sing, their work quickened, they gained on the inflow, and the level began to fall. We would not sink, at any rate! Up ahead the *No. 6*, with an occasional blast of her whistle, pulled for Suva with foaming bows.

There were so many to thank! So many! Captain Nysmyth, who had gone so far beyond his official duty in rendering both technical and spiritual aid; Patrick Ewins, of the *Sigawale*, almost wholly responsible for the manoeuvres of the men in the surf; A. H. Pickmere, of the smart *Arethusa*; Superintendent Sabin and Alexander Bentley and their men; P. T. Tucker and his son, whose home had been our recent headquarters; the men of the Polish *Zjawa*; the Grammar School boys; and, lastly, the men and boys of that remarkable hard-sailing salt-water yacht club of Suva.

Some way off the Public Works Slip the tug let go, and we purposely drifted in to ground on the mud. The hull touched bottom, and with a loud exultant cheer the bailers ceased work, rushed on deck, and swam ashore. It was then that the *Cimba* sank, disappearing entirely from sight.

Grapples were fastened to her; rollers were eased under the sides. When the tide dropped she appeared as though in death, chalk-white, buried in mud. Taggart and I stripped her clean, saving some metal equipment, rope, a few clothes, one or two books, which, together with saturated charts and a few miscellaneous tins, we dried on the shore. When the tide had dropped yet farther a survey of the hull started, a survey which revealed the strength, the integrity, and the honesty of Indian Point ships. True, the false keeling had disappeared; seven strakes had been *rubbed* through by the chafe of coral, and one strake had been pierced. But not a thing more! Not a seam started, not a frame fractured! It was the most incredible fact of the entire voyage!

And yet it appeared that the venture was over. Another

hurricane season was in the offing; the costs of repairing the gutted-out hull, of replacing the lost equipment, could scarcely be met by the slim finances that remained. Yes, we had known this long ago, known it on first striking reef, although somehow we had carried on to this point.

All that afternoon we walked the Lami Road, heedless of the falling rain, ending a long conference in a lurid sunset. Taggart would go, would sacrifice his part in the venture; I would stay and see what could be done.

On the 23rd of September George Taggart, adventurer supreme, brilliant, romantic, who had shown such high courage through thick and thin, made his last gesture to aid the voyage. Weighing twenty pounds less than when joining off Papeete's Quai du Commerce, he boarded an American steamer as a deck-hand, bound for the home he was so soon to leave for gold and the Northern Yukon.

And the moon of that night, showing the town hanging white by quiet water, also showed the old *Cimba* under first repairs, diminutive, unconquered, and impatient for the sea.

NINETEEN

IN A FIJIAN HARBOUR

ONE HOT day in October the *Cimba* was floated with a new keel and planking. Then, as the gutted-out hull would have to be abandoned until after the hurricane season, I went ashore to the home of an inspired builder-designer of flying light-weather craft. Typifying the full integrity of his profession at its best, the wisdom, the long-coursed courage of his sea, Alexander Bentley, gentleman-born, is father to half of Fiji's good shipping. It was with him and his gracious, devoted wife, Lou, that I spent long, happy evenings under a little tin roof in the half-caste quarter, evenings brightened by their good children, by their brother and sister, Maria and Lorry Bentley.

In December the schooner was hove out for coatings of copper paint of Government issue. With masts unshipped and looking the picture of a derelict, she was towed to hurricane moorings in the Waloo Bay swamps. The stormy months descended. Leaving the Bentleys, I voyaged to the Koro Sea islands in the H.M.C.S. *Pioneer* as a guest of her officers, Captain Mullin and Geoffrey Langdale, one of the *Cimba's* dearest friends, boarding on my return at The Gables, atop of Suva, where through months of waiting I was watched over and restrained by those never-to-be-forgotten souls Mrs William Macindoe and her daughter Jean.

Through days of sunshine and shadow . . . bright, white Suva rolling to a green harbour; rainy Suva, with a wind gusty in the heavy trees, the narrow, steep, clean roads; grey Suva, with steaming flower-gardens and jungles, a town of stained slate, pallid under sliding, impenetrable ceilings shifting for the horizon; black Suva, black and with tongues of dazzling sunshine burning fan-shaped over thunderclouds; black with night, flaming with stars—high, white, and cut into imponderable space—as one by one around the harbour shore the drums of Fiji came in from time lost, from the Bay of Islands, from the slopes to Rewa, from the dark rivers of beloved Lami. . . .

By March Suva was once more bright, and there was a general hauling out of shipping, kept from the ways by the long threat of sudden wind. And then every craft coated with Government paint was discovered wormed! Shored above the melancholy backwash of the swamp, the *Cimba* revealed a rotted rudder and post, a fouled stem-piece, the new keel and planks destroyed. The laborious repairs had come to nothing, and now, with her masts out, her cabins emptied and grey, her sides scored by teredos, she appeared ready for the break-up yard at last. But work began, and after many days of effort, infinitely aided by Alexander Bentley, a third keel of hardwood was hauled through the mud and set in place, a new rudder and post fashioned, new strakes bent to the framing. The stem-piece was cleaned and plugged, money was found for paint, which was applied inside and out. I removed the faithless engine, which no longer could be afforded, blocked up the propeller aperture, and after a month and a half in the swamp brought the hull back to the harbour, stepped the masts, and stayed them with new wire rigging.

This was a fair beginning, but only a beginning after all, for now, with resources almost at nil, the craft needed to be entirely re-equipped and stocked. However, no sooner had she cleared the swamp than the problem was forced aside by another. Thanks to the aid of John Bradley, a good friend who had recently stroked a Cambridge crew to a new record, permission had been obtained to ship as a paid crew one Joela, a Fijian boy. The Government had made but one stipulation, merely a formal one, to the effect that the schooner be signed over as a bond for the native. This had been attended to, and the matter appeared settled. But suddenly the officials raised the bond from fifty to sixty pounds, this time demanding a deposit of the sum in full. Not a third of it could be produced. No native could be taken from Fiji without a similar bond; no white man would sail the northern New Guinea route. On the following day a notice came from the immigration authorities to the effect that I must pay a sizable tax for having resided in Fiji for over half a year. Hardly had it been received when a third message arrived, this from the Customs, stating that as the schooner had been in port beyond a six months' limit 20 per cent of her valuation must shortly be paid, failing which, the craft would be seized and sold to obtain the fee.

Taking one thing at a time, I visited all three departments, gaining no ground in the matter of Joela, but finding the Customs and immigration authorities extremely decent and willing to mark time for a short while. I returned aboard, and after hurriedly reaving off halyards and sheets overhauled the old sails, and set to sea to discover whether or not I could cruise without any crew at all. With the *Cimba* lunging white and lean over the horizons, I found myself of a temperament at times suited to the scheme, at times unsuited, but, as I had feared, a shoulder, dislocated some time before and weakened during the wreck, was no longer reliable. Joela had become indispensable! And Joela was lost. Funds dwindled to little more than thirty dollars, the Customs and immigration people served further notice—and the *Cimba* was up for sale.

As some one said, she was a born pilot boat, and before long officials of the Gilberts and New Hebrides were bidding for her by wireless. The sale came as no surprise. Some of the people had been anticipating it right along, a few believed I had suddenly come to see what they chose to call the light, some said that the schooner was a hoodoo, others that her character should bring additional pounds sterling, and still others that she should fetch a high price, if only because she was the smallest vessel to reach the Fijis, and the only one to survive the Suva Reef. And perhaps she would have brought a high price, had I not suddenly received a hundred dollars from home to call off the sale and appeal to the Customs for a last time. Sceptical, but obliging unto the end, they finally gave way, granting a final three weeks of grace, stating that beyond that period the matter could not be kept from the records.

I then set about to retrieve Joela and to meet the bond, equivalent to three times the amount on hand. The first move was to take out a life-insurance policy for a premium of that amount made payable to certain interests, then to sign away a half-ownership in the schooner as a formal guarantee. After appealing to the Secretary of Native Affairs, his

assistant, the Colonial Secretary, and his assistant, Com-
missioner Rata Sacoona, and other officials, I was given permission, with the provision that I stand before a Board of
Trade master-mariner for an examination in celestial navigation, that the schooner be equipped with a rigid tender,
complete navigating equipment, life-saving, and fire-
fighting gear—all to be attended to and accomplished
within the remaining time, now little more than two weeks.

I could not help but sense that these terms represented
hardly more than a nicely turned rejection. However, they
were to be met, and that very day I took a bewildered Joela,
crying through sheer joy, away from the docks to become
the sixth man on the *Cimba's* roster. He was given typhoid
injections, a passport was applied for, a bunk was built for
him in the after-cabin. By great effort some medical supplies, life-rings, waterlights, and two new fire extinguishers
were hurriedly found and put on board. A tender was
thrown together and slung over the stern.

I cleaned and repaired every chart, retrieved the rated
chronometer, and passed without error the tests in navigation before Captain Davidson Hay, spending the final days
of the allotted time bartering for supplies with Suva traders.
And all the while there was no happier, prouder person than
Joela. Serious, eager, smiling, he worked like a slave, with devoted, unflagging spirit. I can see him now, on that last Sunday, straight-backed and short, with a pomp of purple black

hair that no hat in the world could cover, in white shirt-front and cricket coat, his bare feet and legs shiny beneath a neat *sulu*, headed for church, a polished cane in one hand, a large Bible in the other.

Forty-eight hours before the deadline the *Cimba* was ready. Every official term had been met, every cost—with five dollars left over for the New Guinea run. A collection, made by the yacht club under the auspices of the ever-loyal Miss Lotus Sutherland, was not needed, and was gratefully declined. As it was, I would remain under lifelong obligation to that worthy squadron. The call had been a close one, but now, eleven months after the wrecking, the schooner lay in ocean trim, with bins laden with stores, lifelines rigged, the tough Nova Scotian sails ready for service. The Government, finding no further complaint, had remained silent. Only one suspicion hinted that its considerate heads were on second thoughts regretting the approval gained from them: Joela's passport had not been issued. Without it he could not leave; with it he could leave, perhaps into predicaments that would reflect against the conservative official policies at stake. For the week past all inquiries regarding the passport had been evaded. With sailing-time only a matter of hours away, with tension high, with suspicion increasing, I ceased a last-minute task, put on street-clothes, set Joela to tallowing down lanyards, and prepared to discover just how the wind blew. With a final glance at the flawless *Cimba* I stepped ashore—never to board her again. For there on the land I learned the truth. Every preparation had been in vain, every effort wasted: there had been no intention of granting the passport.

THE STEAMER'S first whistle had blown, and the time for leaving had come at last. It pierced a quiet, peaceful night, which until then had been disturbed only by a low wind light with showers, echoing the smothered cries of the Indians under Waimanu Road, the jingle of the mail-boat's winches; a night holding dark the wide harbour, the mountains of unpronounceable names, the waterfront of mist and lamps and sidelights. The schooner and I had parted. There was no blame. Governments—all Governments—are by nature ponderous, for the most part defensive mechanisms, attempting to hide the supreme awkwardness of a bloodless organism by so much negation, diplomacy. No, a Government could not be blamed, and surely not the one of Suva, which had extended more aid and service than had any other on the entire voyage? For months it had offered genuine assistance, and perhaps at the end only inevitably did it lose a flexibility—even as did the venture.

For some while after that final day I lay on my back, first at the Suva Hospital, under the skilled care of Dr McPherson, then at the old Gables, and finally at the Oceanic. When the schooner was taken away I gave only one instruction, and that for the removal of her name-boards.

My friends stood by—Joela, very brave, hiding his despair, Geoffrey Langdale, Alexander Bentley, loyal unto the end, Mrs R. Rutland Bode, Robert Bode, and Jean Macindoe, a courageous, a beautiful spirit of the Fijis.

It was after nearly three months in bed (and after the steamer's final whistle) that I stood on the high deck looking down for a last time at the faces of those friends. I did not wave. A night mist cleared, the warps were hove in, the engine began to thunder, the mahogany railing to vibrate. As I recall, a bugle sounded the sentimental "Farewell to the Islands"—then the crowd slipped into darkness and distance, a little flutter of waving hands, and the steamer, a mountain of metal and light, floated over the harbour. Seventy-five, a hundred yards off her glow caught the form of a small craft. The White 'Un of Nova Scotia, waiting for wind, lay at anchors beneath us. I recalled the best of our last days together; the drives to sea, the runs to Mbenga, to Nukalau; the go with Fahnestocks' *Director*, a sterling Gloucesterman, a run which, called a fisherman's race ashore, was but a single leg with winds in our favour; the victories in local waters over a pair of yawls, both yachts, both larger, and over a forty-five-foot ocean ketch—these seemed the fairest thoughts as I saw her last even as we saw her first, three years before, swaying airy and buoyant as though cut of fragile porcelain on the sea below. . . .

All night long the stars rolled slowly, carefully, across the steamer's masts, and when day broke land had vanished completely. A vast wall of light towered in the east, and the sun had appeared to shine on the scrubbed decks, to burn over the blue and waving spaces of the sea. When it was an hour high a wind came in from the eastern glitter to run fresh over the hush, the sudden hubbub of the ocean, causing the smoke to stand out straight, the sea to roll white. . . . "It's coming now—the wind! Bear a hand! Light out that wingsail; clew out, clew out! She's running eight, she's scudding on her rail, she's dragging her cabin-tops! Here it is—the wind!"